I therefore consider that, in view of the constitution and the laws, the Union is unbroken; and, to the extent of my ability, I shall take care, as the constitution itself expressly enjoins upon me, that the laws of the Union be faithfully executed in all the states.

Doing this I deem to be only a simple duty on my part; and I shall perform it, so far as practicable, unless my rightful masters, the American people, shall withhold the requisite means, or, in some ~~authoritative manner~~ authoritative manner, direct the contrary. I trust this will not be regarded as a menace, but only as the declared purpose of the Union that it will ~~constitutionally~~ constitutionally defend, and maintain itself—

In doing this there needs to be no bloodshed or violence; and there shall be none, unless it be forced upon the national authority. ~~~~

The power confeded to me, will be used to hold, occupy, and possess the property, and places belonging to the government, and to collect the duties and imposts; but beyond what may be necessary for these objects, there will be no invasion— no using of force against, or among the people anywhere. Where hostility to the United States, in any interior locality, shall be so great and so universal, as to prevent competent resident citizens from holding the Federal offices, there will be no attempt to force obnoxious strangers among the people for that object. While the strict legal right may exist in the government to enforce the exercise of these offices, the attempt to do so would be so irritating, and so nearly impracticable with all, that I deem it better to forego, for the time, the uses of such offices.

The mails, unless repelled ~~~~, will continue to be furnished in all parts of the Union. So far as possible, the people everywhere shall have that sense of perfect security which is most favorable to calm thought and reflection.

The course here indicated will be followed, unless current events, and experience, shall show a modification, or change, to be proper; and in every case and exigency, my best discretion will be exercised, according to circumstances actually existing, and with a view and a hope of a peaceful solution of the national troubles, and the restoration of fraternal sympathies and affections.

On becoming

ABRAHAM

LINCOLN

On becoming

ABRAHAM
LINCOLN

From the
1893 BIOGRAPHY

John T. Morse, Jr.

Foreword by
Ronald C. White, Jr.

 LEVENGER
PRESS

Lincoln's student math book consisted of a few sheets of paper that he sewed together. It constitutes the earliest known piece of his writing. He wrote this verse about himself as a student: "Abraham Lincoln/his hand and pen/he will be good but/god knows When."

Published by Levenger Press
420 South Congress Avenue
Delray Beach, Florida 33445 USA
www.Levengerpress.com

First Edition 2008

This work contains Chapters I through VII of the text portion of *Abraham Lincoln* by John T. Morse, Jr., from vol. 1 of 2 volumes, originally published in 1893.

Library of Congress Cataloging-in-Publication Data

Morse, John Torrey, 1840-1937.
  On becoming Abraham Lincoln : from the 1893 biography / John T. Morse,
Jr. ; foreword by Ronald C. White, Jr. -- 1st ed.
        p. cm.
  "This work contains chapters I through VII of the text portion of Abraham
Lincoln by John T. Morse, Jr., from vol. 1 of 2 volumes, originally published in
1893"--T.p. verso.
  ISBN 978-1-929154-33-3
  1. Lincoln, Abraham, 1809-1865. 2. Lincoln, Abraham, 1809-1865--
Childhood and youth. 3. Lincoln, Abraham, 1809-1865--Political career
before 1861. 4. Illinois--Politics and government--To 1865. 5. Legislators--
Illinois--Biography. 6. Presidents--United States--Biography. I. Morse, John
Torrey, 1840-1937. Abraham Lincoln. II. Title.
  E457.3.M67 2008
  973.7092--dc22
  [B]
                                         2008020770

Illustrations by Edward Barbini
Cover and book design by Danielle Furci
Mim Harrison, Editor

With grateful acknowledgment to

A Project of the Illinois Historic Preservation Agency and
the Abraham Lincoln Presidential Library and Museum

CONTENTS

Foreword x

Publisher's Preface xii

I.   The Raw Material 1

II. The Start in Life 23

III. Love; A Duel; Law, and Congress 43

IV. North and South 57

V.   The Lincoln-Douglas Joint Debate 77

VI. Election 111

VII. Interregnum 125

Appendix I. 'A house divided': Letter of February 14, 1860 157
facsimile followed by transcription

Appendix II. Inaugural Address of 1861: Lincoln's final emendations . . 163
facsimile followed by transcription

Sources and Credits 188

Acknowledgments 189

About Our Contributor 190

FOREWORD

As a gentleman-historian from Boston, John T. Morse, Jr. was intrigued by the paradox of Abraham Lincoln's life and thought. How could an uncouth westerner, with almost no formal education, rise to such intellectual and spiritual heights? Morse, a New England Victorian writing at the end of the nineteenth century, actually was asking questions that continue to engage readers at the beginning of the twenty-first century.

Why is it that Lincoln endures? Whereas many renowned eighteenth- or nineteenth-century leaders and writers seem restricted to the past, Lincoln—and his ideas and words—steps across the centuries with the ability to speak to us today. Almost anyone who visits the Lincoln Memorial in Washington is

At critical moments, the nation intuitively returns to Lincoln for words of both healing and determination.

immediately caught up in Lincoln's moral power to inspire each succeeding American generation. His evocation of American ideals, enshrined in the Gettysburg Address and the Second Inaugural Address within that templed space, can touch young people and adults whether it be their first visit or tenth.

Lincoln's legacy is lasting because he embodied what he spoke. Although Morse was careful to present the human side of the young Lincoln, at the center of his artful rendering of Lincoln as statesman was his focus on Lincoln's "close and sympathetic touch with the people." At the bedrock of Lincoln's faith in the people was his own humility. Whereas modern political speeches are suffused with "I," Lincoln virtually disappears in the Gettysburg Address and the Second Inaugural Address. He does not refer to himself once in the Gettysburg Address, and uses the personal pronoun "I" only one time in the Second Inaugural Address. Lincoln pointed away from himself to the principles of the American republic that needed to be renewed in each generation. The audience, then and now, understood that Lincoln was the personification of those principles.

Lincoln's eloquence is his most enduring legacy. His greatest speeches have the timbre of poetry, his words still resonating today. I have discovered that some schoolchildren are beginning to memorize the Gettysburg Address again. I often ask audiences to say aloud Lincoln's benediction from his Second Inaugural Address: "With malice toward none; with charity for all." Lincoln's words of reconciliation, delivered only forty-one days before his death, still speak as an imperative in the present divided world.

The Lincoln who is accessible to us offers his belief in the promise of America. In his own life, and death, he personified the struggle for reconciliation in a nation bitterly divided. If Lincoln is remembered for leading the nation through war, we must not miss the battle within himself. He struggled his whole life over slavery—"If slavery is not wrong, nothing is wrong"—and had to balance his personal views with his oath to the Constitution.

Lincoln remains our most popular president because he is the representative American who is able to paint our highest ideals in word portraits. His words continue to cross all boundaries of time, place, and even language. When communism crumbled in Poland, leaders of the Solidarity Movement came to the United States seeking foundations for their own fledgling democracy. They returned with a Polish anthology of the words of Abraham Lincoln. At critical moments, such as an anniversary of 9/11, the nation intuitively returns to Lincoln for words of both healing and determination.

A man of his time, Lincoln encourages us to define America in our time. Levenger readers should find in Morse's biography a worthy gem that can both inform and inspire today.

– Ronald C. White, Jr.

PUBLISHER'S PREFACE

Biographies of Abraham Lincoln abound. New studies of his presidency are plentiful. Why, then, reprise a portion of a biography first published in 1893?

Precisely because it was.

Our wish is to give readers a sense of Lincoln in his own time, before the twentieth century and then our current one etched new facets into the prism. We read of Lincoln in the language and thinking of his day. In doing so, we experience the history of history.

Today, by virtue of two centuries having passed since Lincoln's birth in 1809, we view the man from afar. But in 1893, he was still within living memory, not yet the icon he would become.

John T. Morse, Jr., the author of this biography, was born in 1840. He was in his twenties when Lincoln held office. Like Lincoln, Morse practiced law. He was also a prolific biographer, editing an ambitious, multi-volume series called *American Statesmen* that included biographies of John Adams, Thomas Jefferson, and Benjamin Franklin. His Lincoln biography was part of *American Statesmen*'s fifth and final series, which covered the Civil War.

Unlike others in the nineteenth century who wrote of Lincoln, and whose works Morse cites—Lincoln's law partner, William Herndon; his friend and bodyguard, Ward Lamon; newspaper editor Dr. Josiah Holland; his friend Congressman Arnold; and his secretaries, John Nicolay and John Hay—Morse was personally removed from Lincoln. He could take a more dispassionate view of the man whose own view, in Morse's words, always focused on "the great main fact." And yet there is in this biography the passion of a writer who sees the greatness of his subject matter.

This is Lincoln in the process of becoming the president of what was not yet a United States of America.

We chose to conclude Morse's biography of Abraham Lincoln with Lincoln's delivery of his first inaugural address. This is Lincoln in the process of becoming the sixteenth president of what was not yet a United States of America, but which Lincoln would irrevocably make so.

But before we encounter this Lincoln, we meet the young student who used a wooden shovel as his palimpsest, whittling down the surface each time he wanted to write something new. The Lincoln who was the abysmal shopkeeper. The one-time postmaster who used his hat as the mail pouch. (Years later, Lincoln's hat became a pouch of a different sort: he used it as the repository for the scraps of paper on which he captured his thoughts for a speech. Then he would literally pull the ideas out of his hat.) There is even the freshly-minted lawyer whose first debates were bombasts of verbosity—long (and best) forgot.

We have also included new material: facsimiles of documents that help show Lincoln in the process of becoming.

"Primarily everything depended upon Abraham Lincoln," observed Morse in his introduction. Morse was referring to Lincoln's role in bringing union to a deeply fissured country. It is a statement that reaches far beyond Lincoln's own time, and that will continue to reach far beyond ours.

On these pages is a glimpse of how it began.

particulars in that instrument; to adjust the subject of representation, to impose taxes on slaves when a system of direct taxation is made, and to perform the duty of surrendering, or causing to be delivered up, fugitive slaves when they escape from the service which they owe in the slave States, and take refuge in the free States. And I am ready to say that if Congress were to attack within the States the institution of slavery, with the purpose of the overthrow or the extinction of slavery, then, Mr. President, "my voice would be for war." Then would be made a case which would justify in the sight of God, and in the presence of the nations of the earth, resistance on the part of the slave States to such an unconstitutional usurped attempt as would be made under the supposition I have stated. Then we should be acting in defence of our rights, of our domicils, of our property, of our safety, of our lives. Then I think would be furnished a case in which the slave States would be justified, by all the considerations which pertain to the happiness or security of man, to employ every instrument which God or nature has placed in our hands, to resist such an attempt upon the part of this Government. Then if, unfortunately, civil war should break out, we should present to the nations of the earth the spectacle of one portion of this Union endeavoring to subvert an institution of another portion, in violation of the Constitution and the most sacred obligations. We should present a spectacle in which we should have the sympathy and good wishes, and desire for our success, of all men who love justice and truth.

Far different would, I fear, be our case, if, unhappily, we should be led into war, into civil war—if the two parts of this country should be placed in a hostile position towards each other in order to carry slavery into new territories acquired from Mexico. Mr. President, we have heard—all of us have read—of the efforts of France to propagate—what, on the continent of Europe? Not slavery, sir, not slavery, but the rights of man; and we know the fate of her efforts of propagandism of that kind. But if, unhappily, we should be involved in war, in civil war, between two parts of this Confederacy, in which the effort upon one side should be to restrain the introduction of slavery into the new territories, and upon the other side to enforce its introduction there, what a spectacle should we present to the astonishment of mankind, in effort, not to propagate rights, but—I must say it, though I trust it will be understood to be said with no design to excite feeling—a war to propagate wrongs in the territories thus

These pages from Lincoln's book of the speeches of Henry Clay show a few markings of Lincoln's in the margins. Early in his political career, Lincoln was an admirer of Clay's and campaigned for Clay's unsuccessful bid of 1844 for the presidency. The book passed into

acquired from Mexico. It would be a war in which we should have no sympathies, no good wishes; in which all mankind would be against us; in which our own history itself would be against us; for, from the commencement of the Revolution down to the present time, we have constantly reproached our British ancestors for the introduction of slavery into this country. And allow me to say that, in my opinion, it is one of the best defences which can be made to preserve the institution of slavery in this country, that it was forced upon us against the wishes of our ancestors—of our own American colonial ancestors—and by the cupidity of our British commercial ancestors.

The power, then, Mr. President, in my opinion—and I extend it to the introduction as well as to the prohibition of slavery in the new territories—does exist in Congress; and I think there is this important distinction between slavery outside of the States and slavery inside of the States; that all outside of the States is debatable, and all inside of the States is not debatable. The Government has no right to attack the institution within the States; but whether she has, and to what extent she has or has not, the right to attack slavery outside of the States, is a debatable question—one upon which men may honorably and fairly differ; and however it may be decided, furnishes I trust, no just occasion for breaking up this glorious Union of ours.

I am not going to take up that part of the subject which relates to the power of Congress to legislate on slavery—I shall have occasion to make some observations upon that subject in the course of my remarks—whether in this District of Columbia or in the Territories; but I must say, in a few words, that I think there are two sources of power, either of which is sufficient, in my judgment, to authorize the exercise of the power either to introduce or keep out slavery, outside of the States and within the Territories. Mr. President, I shall not take up time, of which so much has been consumed already, to show that the clause which gives to Congress the power to make needful rules and regulations respecting the territory and other property of the United States conveys the power to legislate for the Territories. I cannot concur with my worthy friend—and I use the term in its best and most emphatic sense—my friend from Michigan, (MR. CASS) —for I believe we have known each other longer than I have known, and longer than he has known, any other Senator in this hall—I say I cannot concur with that honorable Senator, though I entertain the

39

the hands of Lincoln's friend James W. Somers, who noted in it that Lincoln referred to Clay's speeches when composing his own, early anti-slavery speeches. Other reading that influenced Lincoln early on included Mason Weems's biography of George Washington.

CHAPTER I

THE RAW MATERIAL

Kentucky boyhood home

*"My parents were both born in
Virginia, of undistinguished families…"*

Abraham Lincoln knew little concerning his progenitors, and rested well content with the scantiness of his knowledge. The character and condition of his father, of whom alone upon that side of the house he had personal cognizance, did not encourage him to pry into the obscurity behind that luckless rover. He was sensitive on the subject; and when he was applied to for information, a brief paragraph conveyed all that he knew or desired to know. Without doubt he would have been best pleased to have the world take him solely for himself, with no inquiry as to whence he came,—as if he had dropped upon the planet like a meteorite; as, indeed, many did piously hold that he came a direct gift from heaven. The fullest statement which he ever made was given in December, 1859, to Mr. Fell, who had interrogated him with an eye "to the possibilities of his being an available candidate for the presidency in 1860:" "My parents were both born in Virginia, of undistinguished families,—second families, perhaps I should say. My mother ... was of a family of the name of Hanks, some of whom now remain in Adams, some others in Macon, counties, Illinois. My paternal grandfather, Abraham Lincoln, emigrated from Rockingham County, Virginia, to Kentucky, about 1781 or 1782.... His ancestors, who were Quakers, went to Virginia from Berks County, Pennsylvania. An effort to identify them with the New England family of the same name ended in nothing more definite than a similarity of Christian names in both families, such as Enoch, Levi, Mordecai, Solomon, Abraham, and the like."

*He used to write and to do sums
in arithmetic on the wooden shovel
by the fireside, and to shave off the
surface in order to renew the labor.*

This effort to connect the President with the Lincolns of Massachusetts was afterward carried forward by others, who felt an interest greater than his own in establishing the fact. Yet if he had expected the quest to result satisfactorily, he would probably have been less indifferent about it; for it is obvious that, in common with all Americans of the old native stock, he had a strenuous desire to come of "respectable people;" and his very reluctance to have his apparently low extraction investigated is evidence that he would have been glad to learn that he belonged to an ancient and historical family of the old Puritan Commonwealth, settlers not far from Plymouth Rock, and immigrants not long after the arrival of the Mayflower. This descent has at last been traced by the patient genealogist.

So early as 1848 the first useful step was taken by Hon. Solomon Lincoln of Hingham, Massachusetts, who was struck by a speech delivered by Abraham Lincoln in the national House of Representatives, and wrote to ask facts as to his parentage. The response stated substantially what was afterward sent to Mr. Fell, above quoted. Mr. Solomon Lincoln, however, pursued the search farther, and printed the results. Later, Mr. Samuel Shackford of Chicago, Illinois, himself a descendant from the same original stock, pushed the investigation more persistently. The chain, as put together by these two gentlemen, is as follows: Hingham, Massachusetts, was settled in 1635. In 1636 house lots were set off to Thomas Lincoln, the miller, Thomas Lincoln, the weaver, and Thomas Lincoln, the cooper. In 1638 other lots were set off to Thomas Lincoln, the husbandman, and to Stephen, his brother. In 1637 Samuel Lincoln, aged eighteen, came from England to Salem, Massachusetts, and three years later went to Hingham; he also was a weaver, and a brother of Thomas, the weaver. In 1644 there was a Daniel Lincoln in the place. All these Lincolns are believed to have come from the County of Norfolk in England, though what kinship existed between them is not known. It is from Samuel that the President appears to have been descended. Samuel's fourth son, Mordecai, a blacksmith, married a daughter of Abraham Jones of Hull; about 1704 he moved to the neighboring town of Scituate, and there set up a furnace for smelting iron ore. This couple had six children, of whom two were named respectively Mordecai and Abraham; and these two are believed to have gone to Monmouth County, New Jersey. There Mordecai seems to have continued in the iron business, and later to have made another move to Chester County, Pennsylvania, still continuing in the same business, until, in 1725, he sold out all his "Mynes & Minerals, Forges, etc." Then, migrating again, he settled in

Amity, Philadelphia County, Pennsylvania, where, at last, death caught up with him. By his will, February 22, 1735-36, he bequeathed his land in New Jersey to John, his eldest son; and gave other property to his sons Mordecai and Thomas. He belied the old motto, for in spite of more than three removes he left a fair estate, and in the probate proceedings he is described as "gentleman." In 1748 John sold all he had in New Jersey, and in 1758 moved into Virginia, settling in that part of Augusta County which was afterward set off as Rockingham County. Though his will has not been found, there is "ample proof," says Mr. Shackford, that he had five sons, named Abraham, Isaac, Jacob, Thomas, and John. Of these, Abraham went to North Carolina, there married Mary Shipley, and by her had sons Mordecai, Josiah, and Thomas, who was born in 1778. In 1780 or 1782, as it is variously stated, this family moved to Kentucky. There, one day in 1784, the father, at his labor in the field, was shot by lurking Indians. His oldest son, working hard by, ran to the house for a gun; returning toward the spot where lay his father's body, he saw an Indian in the act of seizing his brother, the little boy named Thomas. He fired, with happy aim; the Indian fell dead, and Thomas escaped to the house. This Thomas it was who afterward became the father of Abraham Lincoln. Of the other sons of Mordecai (great-uncles of the President), Thomas also went to Kentucky, Isaac went to Tennessee, while Jacob and John stayed in Virginia, and begat progeny who became in later times ferocious rebels, and of whom one wrote a very comical blustering letter to his relative the President; and probably another, bearing oddly enough the name of Abraham, was a noted fighter. It is curious to observe of what migratory stock we have here the sketch. Mr. Shackford calls attention to the fact that through six successive generations all save one were "pioneers in the settlement of new countries," thus: 1. Samuel came from England to Hingham, Massachusetts. 2. Mordecai lived and died at Scituate, close by the place of his birth. 3. Mordecai moved, and settled in Pennsylvania, in the neighborhood which afterward became Berks County, while it was still wilderness. 4. John moved into the wilds of Virginia. 5. Abraham went to the backwoods of Kentucky shortly after Boone's settlement. 6. Thomas moved first into the sparsely settled parts of Indiana, and thence went onward to a similar region in Illinois.

Thus in time was corroborated what Abraham Lincoln wrote in 1848 in one of the above-mentioned letters to Hon. Solomon Lincoln: "We have a vague tradition that my great-grandfather went from Pennsylvania to Virginia, and that he was a Quaker." It is of little consequence that this "vague tradition" was stoutly contradicted by the President's father, the ignorant Thomas, who indignantly denied that either a Puritan or a Quaker could be found in the line of his forbears, and who certainly seemed to set heredity at defiance if such were the case. But while thus repudiating others, Thomas himself was in some danger of being repudiated; for so pained have some persons been by the necessity of recognizing Thomas Lincoln as the father of the President, that they have welcomed, as a happy escape from this so miserable paternity, a bit of gratuitous and unsupported gossip, published, though perhaps with more of malice than of faith, by Mr. Herndon, to the effect that Abraham Lincoln was the illegitimate son of some person unknown, presumably some tolerably well-to-do Kentuckian, who induced Thomas to assume the rôle of parent.

There are many stories of fights; others of the lifting of enormous weights; and even some of the doing of great feats of labor in a day, though for such tasks Lincoln had no love. These are not worth recounting.

Upon the mother's side the ancestral showing is meagre, and fortunately so, since the case seems to be a bad one beyond reasonable hope. Her name was Nancy Hanks. She was born in Virginia, and was the illegitimate child of one Lucy Hanks. Nor was she the only instance of illegitimacy in a family which, by all accounts, seems to have been very low in the social scale. Mr. Herndon calls them by the dread name of "poor whites," and gives an unappetizing sketch of them. Throughout his pages and those of Lamon there is abundant and disagreeable evidence to show the correctness of his estimate. Nancy Hanks herself, who certainly was not to blame for her parentage, and perhaps may have improved matters by an infusion of better blood from her unknown father, is described by some as a very rare flower to have bloomed amid the bed of ugly weeds which surrounded her. These friendly writers make her a gentle, lovely,

Christian creature, too delicate long to survive the roughness of frontier life and the fellowship of the shiftless rover to whom she was unfittingly wedded. Whatever she may have been, her picture is exceeding dim, and has been made upon scant and not unquestionable evidence. Mr. Lincoln seems not often to have referred to her; but when he did so it was with expressions of affection for her character and respect for her mental qualities, provided at least that it was really of her, and not of his stepmother, that he was speaking,—a matter not clear from doubt.

On June 10, 1806, Thomas Lincoln gave bond in the "just and full sum of fifty pounds" to marry Nancy Hanks, and two days later, June 12, he did so, in Washington County, Kentucky. She was then twenty-three years old. February 12, 1807, their daughter Sarah was born, who was married and died leaving no issue. February 12, 1809, Abraham Lincoln was born; no other children came save a boy who lived only a few days.

About this time Lincoln ransacked the neighborhood in search of an English grammar, and getting trace of one six miles out from the settlement, he brought it back in triumph, and studied it exhaustively.

The domestic surroundings amid which the babe came into life were wretched in the extreme. All the trustworthy evidence depicts a condition of what civilized people call misery. It is just as well to acknowledge a fact which cannot now be obscured by any amount of euphemism. Yet very many of Lincoln's biographers have been greatly concerned to color this truth, which he himself, with his honest nature, was never willing to misrepresent, however much he resisted efforts to give it a general publicity. He met curious inquiry with reticence, but with no attempt to mislead. Some of his biographers, however, while shunning direct false statements, have used alleviating adjectives with literary skill, and have drawn fanciful pictures of a pious frugal household, of a

gallant frontiersman endowed with a long catalogue of noble qualities, and of a
mother like a Madonna in the wilderness. Yet all the evidence that there is goes
to show that this romantic coloring is purely illusive. Rough, coarse, low,
ignorant, and poverty-stricken surroundings were about the child; and though
we may gladly avail ourselves of the possibility of believing his mother to have
been superior to all the rest of it, yet she could by no means leaven the mass. The
father was by calling a carpenter, but not good at his trade, a shiftless migratory
squatter by invincible tendency, and a very ignorant man, for a long while able
only to form the letters which made his signature, though later he extended his
accomplishments a little. He rested not much above the very bottom of existence
in the pioneer settlements, apparently without capacity or desire to do better.
The family was imbued with the peculiar, intense, but unenlightened form of
Christianity, mingled with curious superstition, prevalent in the backwoods, and
begotten by the influence of the vast wilderness upon illiterate men of a rude
native force. It interests scholars to trace the evolutions of religious faiths, but it
might be not less suggestive to study the retrogression of religion into
superstition. Thomas was as restless in matters of creed as of residence, and made
various changes in both during his life. These were, however, changes without
improvement, and, so far as he was concerned, his son Abraham might have
grown up to be what he himself was contented to remain.

It was in the second year after his marriage that Thomas Lincoln made his
first removal. Four years later he made another. Two or three years afterwards,
in the autumn of 1816, he abandoned Kentucky and went into Indiana. Some
writers have given to this migration the interesting character of a flight from a
slave-cursed society to a land of freedom, but whatever poetic fitness there
might be in such a motive, the suggestion is entirely gratuitous and without the
slightest foundation. In making this move, Thomas's outfit consisted of a
trifling parcel of tools and cooking utensils, with ever so little bedding, and four
hundred gallons of whiskey. At his new quarters he built a "half-faced camp"
fourteen feet square, that is to say, a covered shed of three sides, the fourth side
being left open to the weather. In this, less snug than the winter's cave of a bear,
the family dwelt for a year, and then were translated to the luxury of a "cabin,"
four-walled indeed, but which for a long while had neither floor, door, nor

window. Amid this hardship and wretchedness Nancy Lincoln passed away, October 5, 1818, of that dread and mysterious disease, the scourge of those pioneer communities, known as the "milk-sickness." In a rough coffin, fashioned by her husband "out of green lumber cut with a whip-saw," she was laid away in the forest clearing, and a few months afterward an itinerant preacher performed some funeral rites over the poor woman's humble grave.

For a year Thomas Lincoln was a widower. Then he went back to Kentucky, and found there Mrs. Sally Johnston, a widow, whom, when she was the maiden Sarah Bush, he had loved and courted, and by whom he had been refused. He now asked again, and with better success. The marriage was a little inroad of good luck into his career; for the new wife was thrifty and industrious, with the ambition and the capacity to improve the squalid condition of her husband's household. She had, too, worldly possessions of bedding and furniture, enough to fill a four-horse wagon. She made her husband put a floor, a door, and windows to his cabin. From the day of her advent a new spirit made itself felt amid the belongings of the inefficient Thomas. Her immediate effort was to make her new husband's children "look a little more human," and the youthful Abraham began to get crude notions of the simpler comforts and decencies of life. All agree that she was a stepmother to whose credit it is to be said that she manifested an intelligent kindness towards Abraham.

The opportunities for education were scant enough in that day and place. In his childhood in Kentucky Abraham got a few weeks with one teacher, and then a few weeks with another. Later, in Indiana, he studied a few months, in a scattered way. Probably he had instruction at home, for the sum of all the schooling which he had in his whole life was hardly one year; a singular start upon the road to the presidency of the United States! The books which he saw were few, but a little later he laid hands upon them all and read and re-read them till he must have absorbed all their strong juice into his own nature. Nicolay and Hay give the list: The Bible; "Aesop's Fables;" "Robinson Crusoe;" "The Pilgrim's Progress;" a history of the United States; Weems's "Washington." He was doubtless much older when he devoured the Revised Statutes of Indiana in the office of the town constable. Dr. Holland adds Lives of Henry Clay and of

Franklin (probably the famous autobiography), and Ramsay's "Washington;" and Arnold names Shakespeare and Burns. It was a small library, but nourishing. He used to write and to do sums in arithmetic on the wooden shovel by the fireside, and to shave off the surface in order to renew the labor.

As he passed from boyhood to youth his mental development took its characteristics from the popular demand of the neighborhood. He scribbled verses and satirical prose, wherein the coarse wit was adapted to the taste of the comrades whom it was designed to please; and it must be admitted that, after giving due weight to all ameliorating considerations, it is impossible to avoid disappointment at the grossness of the jesting. No thought, no word raised it above the low level of the audience made up of the laborers on the farms and the loungers in the groceries. The biographer who has made public "The First Chronicles of Reuben" deserves to be held in detestation.

A more satisfactory form of intellectual effervescence consisted in writing articles on the American Government, Temperance, etc., and in speech-making to any who were near at the moment of inspiration. There is abundant evidence, also, that already Lincoln was regarded as a witty fellow, a rare mimic, and teller of jokes and stories; and therefore was the champion of the fields and the favorite of all the primitive social gatherings. This sort of life and popularity had its perils, for in that day and region men seldom met without drinking together; but all authorities are agreed that Lincoln, while the greatest talker, was the smallest drinker.

The stories told of his physical strength rival those which decorate the memory of Hercules. Others, which show his kindly and humane nature, are more valuable. Any or all of these may or may not be true, and, though they are not so poetical or marvelous as the myths which lend an antique charm to the heroes of classic and romantic lore, yet they compare fairly well with those which Weems has twined about the figure of the youthful Washington. There is a tale of the rescue of a pig from a quagmire, and another of the saving of a drunken man from freezing. There are many stories of fights; others of the lifting of enormous weights; and even some of the doing of great feats of labor in a day, though for such tasks Lincoln had no love. These are not worth recounting; there is store of such in every village about the popular local hero; and though historians by such folk-lore may throw a glamour about Lincoln's daily life, he himself, at the time, could hardly have seen much that was romantic or poetical in the routine of ill-paid labor and hard living. Until he came of age his "time" belonged to his father, who let him out to the neighbors for any job that offered, making him a man-of-all-work, without-doors and within. In 1825 he was thus earning six dollars a month, presumably besides board and lodging. Sometimes he slaughtered hogs, at thirty-one cents a day; and in this "rough work" he was esteemed especially efficient. Such was the making of a President in the United States in this nineteenth century!

Thomas Lincoln, like most men of his stamp, had the cheerful habit of laying the results of his own worthlessness to the charge of the conditions about him, which, naturally, he constantly sought to change, since it seemed that no change could bring him to a lower level than he had already found. As Abraham approached his "freedom-day," his luckless parent conceived the notion that he might do better in Illinois than he had done in Indiana. So he shuffled off the farm, for which he had never paid, and about the middle of February the family caravan, with their scanty household wares packed in an ox team, began a march which lasted fourteen days and entailed no small measure of hardship. They finally stopped at a bluff on the north bank of the north fork of the Sangamon, a stream which empties into the Ohio. Here Thomas Lincoln renewed the familiar process of "starting in life," and with an axe, a saw, and a knife built a rough cabin of hewed logs, with a smoke-house and "stable." Abraham, aided by John Hanks, cleared ten or fifteen acres of land, split the rails and fenced it, planted it with corn, and made it over to Thomas as a sort of bequest at the close of his term of legal infancy. His subsequent relationship with his parents, especially with his father, seems to have been slight, involving an occasional gift of money, a very rare visit, and finally a commonplace letter of Christian comfort when the old man was on his deathbed.

At first Abraham's coming of age made no especial change in his condition; he continued to find such jobs as he could, as an example of which is mentioned his bargain with Mrs. Nancy Miller "to split four hundred rails for every yard of brown jeans dyed with white walnut bark that would be necessary to make him a pair of trousers." After many months there arrived in the neighborhood one Denton Offut, one of those scheming, talkative, evanescent busybodies who skim vaguely over new territories. This adventurer had a cargo of hogs, pork, and corn, which he wanted to send to New Orleans, and the engagement fell to Lincoln

His chief trait all his life long was honesty of all kinds; honesty in language, in purpose, in thought; honesty of mind, so that he could never even practice the most tempting of all deceits, a deceit against himself.

and two comrades at the wage of fifty cents per day and a bonus of $60 for the three. It has been said that this and a preceding trip down the Mississippi first gave Lincoln a glimpse of slavery in concrete form, and that the spectacle of negroes "in chains, whipped and scourged," and of a slave auction, implanted in his mind an "unconquerable hate" towards the institution, so that he exclaimed: "If ever I get a chance to hit that thing, I'll hit it hard." So the loquacious myth-maker John Hanks asserts; but Lincoln himself refers his first vivid impression to a later trip, made in 1841, when there were "on board ten or a dozen slaves shackled together with irons." Of this subsequent incident he wrote, fourteen years later, to his friend, Joshua Speed: "That sight was a continual torment to me; and I see something like it every time I touch the Ohio or any other slave border. It is not fair for you to assume that I have no interest in a thing which has, and continually exercises, the power of making me miserable."

Of more immediate consequence was the notion which the rattle-brained Offut conceived of Lincoln's general ability. This lively patron now proposed to build a river steamboat, with "runners for ice and rollers for shoals and dams," of which his redoubtable young employee was to be captain. But this strange scheme gave way to another for opening in New Salem a "general store" of all goods. This small town had been born only a few months before this summer of

1831, and was destined to a brief but riotous life of some seven years' duration. Now it had a dozen or fifteen "houses," of which some had cost only ten dollars for the building; yet to the sanguine Offut it presented a fair field for retail commerce. He accordingly equipped his "store," and being himself engaged in other enterprises, he installed Lincoln as manager. Soon he also gave Lincoln a mill to run.

Vulgarity in itself had no attraction for him;
it simply did not repel him, when with it
there was a flavor of humor or a useful point.

Besides all this patronage, Offut went about the region bragging in his extravagant way that his clerk "knew more than any man in the United States," would some day be President, and could now throw or thrash any man in those parts. Now it so happened that some three miles out from New Salem lay Clary's Grove, the haunt of a gang of frontier ruffians of the familiar type, among whom one Jack Armstrong was champion bully. Offut's boasting soon rendered an encounter between Lincoln and Armstrong inevitable, though Lincoln did his best to avoid it, and declared his aversion to "this woolling and pulling." The wrestling match was arranged, and the settlers flocked to it like Spaniards to a bull-fight. Battle was joined and Lincoln was getting the better of Armstrong, whereupon the "Clary's Grove boys," with fine chivalry, were about to rush in upon Lincoln and maim him, or worse, when the timely intervention of a prominent citizen possibly saved even the life of the future President. Some of the biographers, borrowing the license of poets, have chosen to tell about the "boys" and the wrestling match with such picturesque epithets that the combat bids fair to appear to posterity as romantic as that of Friar Tuck and Robin Hood. Its consequence was that Armstrong and Lincoln were fast friends ever after. Wherever Lincoln was at work, Armstrong used to "do his loafing," and Lincoln made visits to Clary's Grove, and long afterward did a friendly service to "old Hannah," Armstrong's wife, by saving one of her vicious race from the gallows, which upon that especial occasion he did not happen to deserve. Also Armstrong and his gang gave Lincoln hearty political support, and an assistance at the polls which was very effective, for success generally smiled on that candidate who had as his constituency the "butcher-knife boys," the "barefooted boys," the "half-horse, half-alligator men," and the "huge-pawed boys."

An item less susceptible of a poetic coloring is that about this time Lincoln ransacked the neighborhood in search of an English grammar, and getting trace of one six miles out from the settlement, he walked over to borrow or to buy it. He brought it back in triumph, and studied it exhaustively.

There are also some tales of his honesty which may stand without disgrace beside that of Washington and the cherry-tree, and may be better entitled to credit. It is said that, while he was "keeping shop" for Offut, a woman one day accidentally overpaid him by the sum of fourpence, and that he walked several miles that night to restore the sum to her before he slept. On another occasion, discovering that in selling half a pound of tea he had used too small a weight, he started instantly forth to make good the deficiency. Perhaps this integrity does not so much differentiate Lincoln from his fellows as it may seem to do, for it is said that honesty was the one distinguishing virtue of that queer society. None the less these legends are exponents, which the numerous fighting stories are not, of the genuine nature of the man. His chief trait all his life long was honesty of all kinds and in all things; not only commonplace, material honesty in dealings, but honesty in language, in purpose, in thought; *honesty of mind*, so that he could never even practice the most tempting of all deceits, a deceit against himself. This pervasive honesty was the trait of his identity, which stayed with him from beginning to end, when other traits seemed to be changing, appearing or disappearing, and bewildering the observer of his career. All the while the universal honesty was there.

It took less than a year for Offut's shop to come to ruin, for the proprietor to wander off into the unknown void from which he had come, and for Lincoln to find himself again without occupation. He won some local reputation by navigating the steamboat Talisman up the Sangamon River to Springfield; but nothing came of it.

The foregoing narrative ought to have given some idea of the moral and physical surroundings of Lincoln's early days. Americans need to carry their memories hardly fifty years back, in order to have a lively conception of that peculiar body of men which for many years was pushed out in front of civilization in the West. Waifs and strays from highly civilized communities, these wanderers had not civilization to learn, but rather they had shuffled off much that belonged to civilization, and afterwards they had to acquire it afresh. Among them crudity in thought and uncouthness in habits were intertwined in odd, incongruous crossings with the remnants of the more respectable customs with which they had once been familiar. Much they forgot and much they put away as being no longer useful; many of them—not all—became very ignorant without being stupid, very brutal without being barbarous. Finding life hard, they helped each other with a general kindliness which is impracticable among the complexities of elaborate social organizations. Those who were born on the land, among whom Lincoln belonged, were peculiar in having no reminiscences, no antecedent ideas derived from their own past, whereby to modify the influences of the immediate present. What they should think about men and things they gathered from what they saw and heard around them. Even the modification to be got from reading was of the slightest, for very little reading was possible, even if desired. An important trait of these Western communities was the closeness of personal intercourse in them, and the utter lack of any kind of barriers establishing strata of society. Individuals might differ ever so widely; but the wisest and the dullest, the most worthless and the most enterprising, had to rub shoulder to shoulder in daily life. Yet the variety was considerable: hardy and danger-loving pioneers fulfilling the requirements of romance; shiftless vagrants curiously combining utter inefficiency with a sort of bastard contempt for hardship; ruffians who could only offset against every brutal vice an ignoble physical courage; intelligent men whose observant eyes ranged over the whole region in a shrewd search after enterprise and profit; a few educated men, decent in apparel and bearing, useful in legislation and in preventing the ideal from becoming altogether vulgarized and debased; and others whose energy was chiefly of the tongue, the class imbued with a taste for small politics and the public business. All these and many other varieties were like ingredients cast together into a caldron; they could not keep apart, each with his own kind, to the degree which is customary in old established communities; but they all ceaselessly crossed and mingled and met, and talked, and dealt, and helped and hustled each other, and exerted upon each other that subtle inevitable influence resulting from such constant intercourse; and so they inoculated each other with certain characteristics which became common to all and formed the type of the early settler. Thus was made "the new West," "the great West," which was pushed ever onward, and endured along each successive frontier for about a generation. An eternal movement, a tireless coming and going, pervaded these men; they passed hither and thither without pause, phantasmagorically; they seemed to be forever "moving on," some because they were real pioneers and

Law and politics stimulated and educated the settlers in a way that only Americans can appreciate. When Lincoln turned to them, he turned to the highest callings which could tempt intellect and ambition.

natural rovers, others because they were mere vagrants generally drifting away from creditors, others because the better chance seemed ever in the newer place, and all because they had struck no roots, gathered no associations, no home ties, no local belongings. The shopkeeper "moved on" when his notes became too pressing; the schoolmaster, after a short stay, left his school to some successor whose accomplishments could hardly be less than his own; clergymen ranged vaguely through the country, to preach, to pray, to bury, to marry, as the case might be; farmers heard of a more fruitful soil, and went to seek it. Men certainly had at times to work hard in order to live at all, yet it was perfectly possible for the natural idler to rove, to loaf, and to be shiftless at intervals, and to become as demoralized as the tramp for whom a shirt and trousers are the sum of worldly possessions. Books were scarce; many teachers hardly had as much book-learning as lads of thirteen years now have among ourselves. Men who could neither read nor write abounded, and a deficiency so common could hardly imply much disgrace or a marked inferiority; many learned these difficult arts only in mature years. Fighting was a common pastime, and when these rough fellows fought, they fought like savages; Lincoln's father bit off his adversary's nose in a fight, and a cousin lost the same feature in the same way; the "gouging" of eyes was a legitimate resource. The necessity of fighting might at any moment come to any one; even the combination of a peaceable disposition with formidable strength did not save Lincoln from numerous personal affrays, of which many are remembered, and not improbably many more have been forgotten. In spite of the picturesque adjectives which have been so decoratively used in describing the ruffian of the frontier, he seems to have been about what his class always is; and when these fellows had forced a fight, or "set up" a match, their chivalry never prevented any unfairness or brutality. A tale illustrative of the times is told of a closely contested election in the legislature for the office of state treasurer. The worsted candidate strode into the hall of the Assembly, and gallantly selecting four of the largest and strongest of those who had voted against him, thrashed them soundly. The other legislators ran away. But before the close of the session this pugilist, who so well understood practical politics, was appointed clerk of the Circuit Court and county recorder.

Corn bread was the chief article of diet; potatoes were a luxury, and were often eaten raw like apples. To the people at large whiskey "straight" seemed the natural drink of man, and whiskey toddy was not distasteful to woman. To refuse to drink was to subject one's self to abuse and suspicion; Lincoln's notorious lack of liking for it passed for an eccentricity, or a physical peculiarity. The customary social gatherings were at horse-racings, at corn-shuckings, at political speech-makings, at weddings, whereat the coarse proceedings would not nowadays bear recital; at log-rollings, where the neighbors gathered to collect the logs of a newly cleared lot for burning; and at house-raisings, where they kindly aided to set up the frame of a cabin for a new-comer; at camp-meetings, where the hysterical excitement of a community whose religion was more than half superstition found clamorous and painful vent; or perchance at a hanging, which, if it met public approbation, would be sanctioned by the gathering of the neighbors within a day's journey of the scene. At dancingparties men and women danced barefoot; indeed, they could hardly do better, since their foot-wear was apt to be either moccasins, or such boots as they themselves could make from the hides which they themselves had cured. In Lincoln's boyhood the hunting-shirt and leggings made of skins were a sufficiently respectable garb; and buckskin breeches dyed green were enough to captivate the heart of any girl who wished a fashionable lover; but by the time that he had become a young man, most self-respecting men had suits of jeans. The ugly butcher's knife and tomahawk, which had been essential as was the rapier to the costume of gentlemen two centuries earlier, began now to be more rarely seen at the belt about the waist. The women wore linsey-woolsey gowns, of home manufacture, and dyed according to the taste or skill of the wearer in stripes and bars with the brown juice of the butternut. In the towns it was not long before calico was seen, and calfskin shoes; and in such populous centres bonnets decorated the heads of the fair sex. Amid these advances in the art of dress Lincoln was a laggard, being usually one of the worst attired men of the neighborhood; not from affectation, but from a natural indifference to such matters. The sketch is likely to become classical in American history of the appearance which he presented with his scant pair of trousers, "hitched" by a single suspender over his shirt, and so short as to expose, at the lower end, half a dozen inches of "shinbone, sharp, blue, and narrow."

In the clearings the dwellings of these men were the "half-faced camp" open upon one side to the weather, or the doorless, floorless, and windowless cabin which, with prosperity, might be made luxurious by greased paper in the windows, and "puncheon" floors. The furniture was in keeping with this exterior. At a corner the bed was constructed by driving into the ground crotched sticks, whence poles extended to the crevices of the walls; upon these poles were laid boards, and upon these boards were tossed leaves and skins and such other alleviating material as could be found. Three-legged stools and a table were hewed from the felled trees with an axe, which was often the settler's only and invaluable tool, and which he would travel long miles to sharpen. If a woman wanted a looking-glass, she scoured a tin pan, but the temptation to inspect one's self must have been feeble. A very few kitchen utensils completed the outfit. Troughs served for washtubs, when washtubs were used; and wooden ploughs broke up the virgin soil. The whole was little, if at all, more comfortable than the red man's wigwam. In "towns," so called, there was of course somewhat more of civilization than in the clearings. But one must not be misled by a name; a "town" might signify only a score of houses, and the length of its life was wholly problematical; a few days sufficed to build the wooden huts, which in a few years might be abandoned. In the early days there was almost no money among the people; sometimes barter was resorted to; one lover paid for his marriage license with maple sugar, another with wolf-scalps. More often a promise sufficed; credit was a system well understood, and promissory notes constituted an unquestioned and popular method of payment that would have made a millennium for Mr. Micawber. But however scant might be cash

The very quality which made Lincoln, as a young man, not much superior to his coarse surroundings was precisely the same quality which made him what he was in later life.

and houses, each town had its grocery, and these famous "stores" were by far the chief influence in shaping the ideas of the Westerner. There all congregated, the idlers all day long, the busy men in the evening; and there, stimulated by the whiskey of the proprietor, they gossiped about everybody's affairs, talked about business and the prospects of the neighborhood, and argued about the politics of the county, the State, and even of the nation. Jokes and stories, often most uncouth and gross, whiled away the time. It was in these groceries, and in the rough crucible of such talk, wherein grotesque imagery and extravagant phrases were used to ridicule pretension and to bring every man to his place, sometimes also to escape taking a hard fact too hardly, that what we now call "American humor," with its peculiar native flavor, was born. To this it is matter of tradition that Lincoln contributed liberally. He liked neighborly chat and discussion; and his fondness for political debate, and his gifts in tale and jest, made him the most popular man in every "store" that he entered. It is commonly believed that the effect of this familiarity with coarse talk did not afterward disappear, so that he never became fastidious in language or in story. But apologists of this habit are doubtless correct in saying that vulgarity in itself had no attraction for him; it simply did not repel him, when with it there was a flavor of humor or a useful point. Apparently it simply meant nothing to him; a mental attitude which is not difficult of comprehension in view of its origin.

Some of the most picturesque and amusing pages of Ford's "History of Illinois" describe the condition of the bench and bar of these times. "Boys, come in, our John is going to hold court," proclaimed the sheriff; and the "boys" loitered into the barroom of the tavern, or into a log cabin where the judge sat on the bed and thus, really from the woolsack, administered "law" mixed with equity as best he knew it. Usually these magistrates were prudent in guiding the course of practical justice, and rarely summed up the facts lest they should make dangerous enemies, especially in criminal cases; they often refused to state the law, and generally for a very good reason. They liked best to turn the whole matter over to the jurors, who doubtless "understood the case, and would do justice between the parties." The books of the science were scarce, and lawyers who studied them were perhaps scarcer. But probably substantial fairness in decision did not suffer by reason of lack of sheepskin learning.

Politics for a long while were strictly personal; the elections did not turn upon principles or measures, but upon the popular estimate of the candidates individually. Political discussion meant unstinted praise and unbounded vilification. A man might, if he chose, resent a vote against himself as a personal insult, and hence arose much secrecy and the "keep dark" system. Stump-speaking, whiskey, and fighting were the chief elements of a campaign, and the worst class in society furnished the most efficient backing.

Such was the condition of men and things in the neighborhood where Abraham Lincoln was shaping in the days of his youth. Yet it was a condition which did not last long; Illinois herself changed and grew as rapidly as any youngster within her borders. The rate of advance in all that goes to make up what we now regard as a civilized society was astonishing. Between the time when Lincoln was fifteen and when he was twenty-five, the alteration was so great as to be confusing. One hardly became familiar with a condition before it had vanished. Some towns began to acquire an aspect of permanence; clothes and manners became like those prevalent in older communities, many men were settling down in established residence, identifying themselves with the fortunes of their neighborhood. Young persons were growing up and staying where they had been "raised," as the phrase of a farming community had it. Comfortable and presentable two-story houses lent an air of prosperity and stimulated ambition; law-books began to be collected in small numbers; and debts were occasionally paid in money, and could often be collected by legal process. These improvements were largely due to the swelling tide of immigration which brought men of a better type to push their enterprises in a country presumably emerging from its disagreeable stage. But the chief educational influence was to be found in the Anglo-American passion for an argument and a speech. Hand in hand, as has so long been the custom in our country, law and politics moved among the people, who had an inborn, inherited taste for both; these stimulated and educated the settlers in a way that only Americans can appreciate. When Lincoln, as is soon to be seen, turned to them, he turned to what then and there appeared the highest callings which could tempt intellect and ambition.

The preëminently striking feature in Lincoln's nature—not a trait of character, but a characteristic of the man—which is noteworthy in these early days, and grew more so to the very latest, was the extraordinary degree to which he always appeared to be in close and sympathetic touch with the people, that is to say, the people in the mass wherein he was imbedded, the social body amid which he dwelt, which pressed upon him on all sides, which for him formed "the public." First this group or body was only the population of the frontier settlement; then it widened to include the State of Illinois; then it expanded to the population of the entire North; and such had come to be the popular appreciation of this remarkably developed quality that, at the time of his death, his admirers even dared to believe that it would be able to make itself one with all the heterogeneous, discordant, antagonistic elements which then composed the very disunited United States. It is by reason of this quality that it has seemed necessary to depict so far as possible that peculiar, transitory phase of society which surrounded his early days. This quality in him caused him to be exceptionally susceptible to the peculiar influences of the people among whom his lot was cast. This quality for a while prevented his differentiating himself from them, prevented his accepting standards and purposes unlike theirs either in speech or action, prevented his rising rapidly to a higher moral plane than theirs. This quality kept him essentially one of them, until his "people" and his "public" expanded beyond them. It has been the fashion of his admirers to manifest an extreme distaste for a truthful presentation of his earlier days. Some writers have passed very lightly over them; others, stating plain facts with a formal accuracy, have used their skill to give to the picture an untruthful miscoloring; two or three, instinct with the spirit of Zola, have made their sketch with plain unsparing realism in color as well as in lines, and so have brought upon themselves abuse, and perhaps have deserved much of it, by

His day and generation uttered itself through him.

reason of a lack of skill in doing an unwelcome thing, or rather by reason of overdoing it. The feeling which has led to suppression or to a falsely romantic description seems to me unreasonable and wrong. The very quality which made Lincoln, as a young man, not much superior to his coarse surroundings was precisely the same quality which, ripening and expanding rapidly and grandly with maturing years and a greater circle of humanity, made him what he was in later life. It is through this quality that we get continuity in him; without it, we cannot evade the insoluble problem of two men,—two lives,—one following the other with no visible link of connection between them; without it we have physically one creature, morally and mentally two beings. If we reject this trait, we throw away the only key which unlocks the problem of the most singular life, taken from end to end, which has ever been witnessed among men, a life which many have been content to regard as an unsolved enigma. But if we admit and really perceive and feel the full force of this trait, developed in him in a degree probably unequaled in the annals of men, then, besides the enlightenment which it brings, we have the great satisfaction of eliminating much of the disagreeableness attendant upon his youthful days. Even the commonness and painful coarseness of his foolish written expressions become actually an exponent of his chief and crowning quality, his receptiveness and his expression of humanity,—that is to say, of all the humanity he then knew. At first he expressed what he could discern with the limited, inexperienced vision of the ignorant son of a wretched vagrant pioneer; later he gave expression to the humanity of a people engaged in a purpose physically and morally as vast and as grand as any enterprise which the world has seen. Thus, with perfect fairness, without wrenching or misrepresentation or sophistry, the ugliness of his youth ceases to be his own and becomes only the presentation of a curious social condition. In his youth he expressed a low condition, in later life a noble one; at each period he expressed correctly what he found. His day and generation uttered itself through him. With such thoughts, and from this point of view, it is possible to contemplate Lincoln's early days, amid all their degraded surroundings and influences and unmarked by apparent antagonism or obvious superiority on his part, without serious dismay.

CHAPTER II

THE START IN LIFE

The Berry-Lincoln General Store

*"…considering the great probability that the
framers of those laws were wiser than myself,
I should prefer not meddling with them."*

In Illinois during the years of Lincoln's boyhood the red man was retiring sullenly before the fatal advance of the white man's frontier. Shooting, scalping, and plundering forays still occurred, and in the self-complaisant reminiscences of the old settlers of that day the merciless and mysterious savage is apt to lend to the narrative the lively coloring of mortal danger. In the spring of 1832 a noted chief of the Sacs led a campaign of such importance that it lives in history under the dignified title of "the Black Hawk war." The Indians gathered in numbers so formidable that Governor Reynolds issued a call for volunteers to aid the national forces. Lincoln, left unemployed by the failure of Offut, at once enlisted. The custom then was, so soon as there were enough recruits for a company, to elect a captain by vote. The method was simple: each candidate stood at some point in the field and the men went over to one or another according to their several preferences. Three fourths of the company to which Lincoln belonged ranged themselves with him, and long afterward he used to say that no other success in life had given him such pleasure as did this one.

The company was attached to the Fourth Illinois Regiment, commanded by Colonel Samuel Thompson, in the brigade of General Samuel Whiteside. On April 27 they started for the scene of conflict, and for many days endured much hardship of hunger and rough marching. But thereby they escaped serious danger, for they were too fatigued to go forward on May 12, when the cavalry battalions rode out gallantly, recklessly, perhaps a little stupidly, into ambush and death. It so happened that Lincoln never came nearer to any engagement than he did to this one of "Stillman's Run;" so that in place of military glory he had to be content with the reputation of being the best comrade and story-teller at the camp fire. He had, however, an opportunity to do one honorable act: the brief term of service of the volunteers expired on May 27, and most of them eagerly hastened away from an irksome task, without regard to the fact that their services were still much needed, whereas Lincoln and some other officers reënlisted as privates. They were made the "Independent Spy Battalion" of mounted volunteers, were given many special privileges, but were concerned in no engagement, and erelong were mustered out of service. Lincoln's certificate of discharge was signed by Robert Anderson, who afterward was in command at Fort Sumter at the outbreak of the rebellion. Thus, late in June, Lincoln was again a civilian in New Salem, and was passing from war to politics.

Nomination by caucus had not yet been introduced into Illinois, and any person who wished to be a candidate for an elective office simply made public announcement of the fact and then conducted his campaign as best he could. On March 9, 1832, shortly before his enlistment, Lincoln issued a manifesto "To the People of Sangamon County," in which he informed them that he should run as a candidate for the state legislature at the autumn elections, and told them his political principles. He was in favor of internal improvements, such as opening roads, clearing streams, building a railroad across Sangamon

He spoke also for a national bank and a high protective tariff; probably he knew very little about either.

County, and making the Sangamon River straight and navigable. He advocated a usury law, and hazarded the extraordinary argument that "in cases of extreme necessity there could always be means found to cheat the law; while in all other cases it would have its intended effect." A law ameliorated by infractions is no uncommon thing, but this is perhaps the only instance in which a law has been befriended on the ground that it can be circumvented. He believed that every man should "receive at least a moderate education." He deprecated changes in existing laws; for, he said, "considering the great probability that the framers of those laws were wiser than myself, I should prefer not meddling with them." The clumsy phraseology of his closing paragraph coupled not badly a frank avowal of ambition with an ingenuous expression of personal modesty. The principles thus set forth were those of Clay and the Whigs, and at this time the "best people" in Sangamon County belonged to this party. The Democrats, on the other hand, did not much concern themselves with principles, but accepted General Jackson in place thereof, as constituting in himself a party platform. In the rough-and-tumble pioneer community they could not do better, and for many years they had controlled the State; indeed, Lincoln himself had felt no small loyalty towards a President who admirably expressed Western civilization. Now, however, he considered himself "an avowed Clay man," and besides the internal improvement system he spoke also for a national bank and a high protective tariff; probably he knew very little about either, but his partisanship was perfect, for if there was any distinguishing badge of an anti-Jackson Whig, it certainly was advocacy of a national bank.

*One of his friends was getting roughly
handled, whereupon Lincoln, descending
from the rostrum, took a hand in the affray,
tossed one of the assailants "ten or twelve feet
easily," and then continued his harangue.*

After his return from the "war," Lincoln set about electioneering with a good show of energy. He hardly anticipated success, but at least upon this trial trip he expected to make himself known to the people and to gain useful experience. He "stumped" his own county thoroughly, and is said to have made speeches which were blunt, crude, and inartificial, but not displeasing to his audiences. A story goes that once "a general fight" broke out among his hearers, and one of his friends was getting roughly handled, whereupon Lincoln, descending from the rostrum, took a hand in the affray, tossed one of the assailants "ten or twelve feet easily," and then continued his harangue. Yet not even thus could he win, and another was chosen over his head. He had, however, more reason to be gratified than disappointed with the result; for, though in plain fact he was a raw and unknown youngster, he stood third upon a list of eight candidates, receiving 657 votes; and out of 208 votes cast in his own county he scored 205. In this there was ample encouragement for the future.

The political campaign being over, and legislative functions postponed, Lincoln was brought face to face with the pecuniary problem. He contemplated, not without approbation, the calling of the blacksmith; but the chance to obtain a part interest in a grocery "store" tempted him into an occupation for which he was little fitted. He became junior partner in the firm of Berry & Lincoln, which, by executing and delivering sundry notes of hand, absorbed the whole grocery business of the town. But Lincoln was hopelessly inefficient behind the counter, and Berry was a tippler. So in a year's time the store "winked out," leaving as its only important trace those ill-starred scraps of paper by which it had been founded. Berry "moved on" from the inconvenient neighborhood, and soon afterward died, contributing nothing to reduce the indebtedness. Lincoln patiently continued to make payments during several years to come, until he had discharged the whole amount. It was only a few hundred dollars, but to him it seemed so enormous that betwixt jest and earnest he called it "the national debt." So late as in 1848, when he was a member of the House of Representatives at Washington, he applied part of his salary to this old indebtedness.

During this "store"-keeping episode he had begun to study law, and while "keeping shop" he was with greater diligence reading Blackstone and such other elementary classics of the profession as he could borrow. He studied with zeal and became absorbed in his books. Perched upon a woodpile, or lying under a tree with his feet thrust upwards against the trunk and "grinding around with the shade," he caused some neighbors to laugh uproariously, and others to say that he was daft. In fact, he was in grim earnest, and held on his way with much persistence.

May 7, 1833, Lincoln was commissioned as postmaster at New Salem. His method of distributing the scanty mail was to put all the letters in his hat, and to hand them out as he happened to meet the persons to whom they were addressed. The emoluments could hardly have gone far towards the discharge of "the national debt." His incumbency in this office led to a story worth telling. When New Salem, and by necessity also the post-office, like the grocery shop, "winked out," in 1836, there was a trifling balance of sixteen or eighteen dollars due from Lincoln to the government. Several years afterward, when he was practicing law in Springfield, the government agent at last appeared to demand a settlement. Lincoln went to his trunk and drew forth "an old blue sock with a quantity of silver and copper coin tied up in it," the identical bits of money which he had gathered from the people at New Salem, and which, through many days of need in the long intervening period, he had not once touched.

Fortunately an occupation now offered itself which was more lucrative, and possessed also the valuable quality of leaving niches of leisure for the study of the law. The mania for speculation in land had begun in Illinois; great tracts were being cut up into "town lots," and there was as lively a market for real estate as the world has ever seen. The official surveyor of the county, John Calhoun, had more work than he could do, and offered to appoint Lincoln as a deputy. A little study made him competent for the work, which he performed for some time with admirable accuracy, if the stories are to be believed. But he had not long enjoyed the mild prosperity of this new career ere an untoward interruption came from a creditor of the extinct grocery firm. This man held one of the notes representing "the national debt," and now levied execution

At this session he first saw Stephen A. Douglas, then a lobbyist, and said of him: "He is the least man I ever saw."

upon Lincoln's horse and surveying instruments. Two friends, however, were at hand in this hour of need, and Bolin Greene and James Short are gratefully remembered as the men who generously furnished, in that actual cash which was so scarce in Illinois, the sums of one hundred and twenty-five dollars and one hundred and twenty dollars respectively, to redeem these essential implements of Lincoln's business.

The summer of 1834 found Lincoln again a candidate for the legislature. He ran as a Whig, but he received and accepted offers of aid from the Democrats, and their votes swelled the flattering measure of his success. It has usually been stated that he led the four successful candidates, the poll standing: Lincoln, 1,376; Dawson, 1,370; Carpenter, 1,170; Stuart, 1,164. But Mr. Herndon adduces evidence that Dawson's number was 1,390, whereby Lincoln is relegated to the second place. Holland tells us that he "shouldered his pack and on foot trudged to Vandalia, then the capital of the State, about a hundred miles, to make his entrance into public life." But the correcting pen of the later biographer interferes with this dramatic incident also. For it seems that, after the result of the election was known, Lincoln visited a friend, Coleman Smoot, and said: "Did you vote for me?" "I did," replied Smoot. "Then," said Lincoln, "you must lend me two hundred dollars!" This seemed a peculiar *sequitur*, for ordinary political logic would have made any money that was to pass between voter and candidate move the other way. Yet Smoot accepted the consequence entailed in part by his own act, and furnished the money, whereby Lincoln was able to purchase a new suit of clothes and to ride in the stage to Vandalia.

The records of this legislature show nothing noteworthy. Lincoln was very inappropriately placed on the Committee on Public Accounts and Expenditures; also it is recorded that he introduced a resolution to obtain for the State a part of the proceeds of the public lands sold within it. What has chiefly interested the chroniclers is, that at this session he first saw Stephen A. Douglas, then a lobbyist, and said of him: "He is the least man I ever saw." Lincoln's part seems to have been rather that of an observer than of an actor. The account given is that he was watching, learning, making acquaintances, prudently preparing for future success, rather than endeavoring to seize it too greedily. In fact, there is reason to believe that his thoughts were intent on far other matter than the shaping of laws and statutes. For to this period belongs the episode of Ann Rutledge. The two biographers whose personal knowledge is the best regard this as the one real romance of Lincoln's life. Heretofore he had held himself shyly aloof from women's society, but this maiden won his heart. She comes before posterity amid a glamour of rhetorical description, which attributes to her every grace of form and feature, every charm of character and intellect. She was but a schoolgirl of seventeen years when two men became her lovers; a year or more afterward she became engaged to one of them, but before they could be married he made a somewhat singular excuse for going to New York on family affairs. His absence was prolonged and his letters became few. People said that the girl had been deceived, and Lincoln began to hope that the way was clearing for him. But under the prolonged strain Miss

Rutledge's health broke down, and on August 25, 1835, she died of brain fever. Lincoln was allowed to see her as she lay near her end. The effect upon him was grievous. Many declared him crazy, and his friends feared that he might go so far as to take his own life; they watched him closely, and one of them at last kindly took him away from the scene of his sufferings for a while, and bore him constant and cheering company. In time the cloud passed, but it seems certain

He was afflicted sorely with a constitutional tendency to gloom. Like a dark fog-bank it hung, always dull and threatening, on the verge of his horizon, never wholly disappearing.

that on only one or two other occasions in his life did that deep melancholy, which formed a permanent background to his temperament, take such overmastering, such alarming and merciless possession of him. He was afflicted sorely with a constitutional tendency to gloom, and the evil haunted him all his life long. Like a dark fog-bank it hung, always dull and threatening, on the verge of his horizon, sometimes rolling heavily down upon him, sometimes drawing off into a more or less remote distance, but never wholly disappearing. Every one saw it in his face and often felt it in his manner, and few pictures of him have been made so bad as not in some degree to present it. The access of it which was brought on by this unhappy love affair was somewhat odd and uncouth in its manifestations, but was so genuine and sincere that one feels that he was truly undergoing the baptism of a great sorrow.

At no other point is there more occasion to note this trait of character, which presents a curious and interesting subject for study. Probably no exhaustive solution is possible. One wanders off into the mystery of human nature, loses his way in the dimness of that which can be felt but cannot be expressed, and becomes aware of even dimmer regions beyond in which it is vain to grope. It is well known that the coarse and rough side of life among the pioneers had its reaction in a reserved and at times morose habit, nearly akin to sadness, at least in those who frequented the wilderness; it was the expression of the influence of the vast, desolate, and lonely nature amid which they passed their lives. It is true that Lincoln was never a backwoodsman, and never roved alone for long periods among the shadowy forests and the limit-less prairies, so that their powerful and weird influences, though not altogether remote, never bore upon him in full force; yet their effect was everywhere around him, and through others he imbibed it, for his disposition was sensitive and sympathetic for such purposes. That there was also a simple prosaic physical inducement cannot be denied. Hardship and daily discomfort in all the arrangements of life counted for something, and especially so the bad food, greasy, unwholesome, horribly cooked, enough to afflict an ostrich with the blue devils of dyspepsia. The denizen of the town devoured messes vastly worse than the simple meal of the hunter and trapper, and did not counteract the ill effect by hard exercise in the free, inspiring air. Such facts must be considered, though they diminish the poetry which rhetoricians and sentimentalists have cast over the melancholy of Lincoln's temperament. Yet they fall far short of wholly accounting for a gloom which many have loved to attribute to the mysticism of a great destiny, as though the awful weight of his immense task was making itself felt in his strange, brooding nature long years before any human prophet could have forecast any part of that which was to come. In this apparent vague consciousness of the oppression of a great burden of toil, duty, and responsibility, casting its shadow so far before, there is something so fascinating to the imagination of man that we cannot quite forego it, or accept any explanation which would compel us altogether to part with it. The shuddering awe and terrible sense of fate, which the grandeur of the Greek tragedies so powerfully expresses, come to us when we contemplate this strange cloud which never left Lincoln in any year after his earliest youth, although some traits in his character seemed often incomprehensibly to violate it, and like rebellious spirits to do outrage to it, while, in fact, they only made it the more striking, picturesque, and mysterious. But, after all explanations have been made, the conclusion must be that there is no one and only thread to guide us through the labyrinth to the heart of this singular trait, and each of us must follow that which his own nature renders intelligible or congenial for him. To us, who know the awful closing acts of his life-drama, it seems so appropriate that there should be an impressive unity, and so an inevitable backward influence working from the end towards the beginning, that we cannot avoid, nor would avoid, an instinctive belief that an occult moral and mental condition already existed in the years of Lincoln's life which we are now observing, although the profound cause of that condition lay wholly in the future, in the years which were still far away. There is a charm in the very unreason and mysticism of such a faith, and mankind will never quite fail to fancy, if not actually to believe, that the life which Lincoln had to live in the future wrought in some inexplicable way upon the life which he was living in the present. The explanation is not more strange than the enigma.

Returning now to the narrative, an unpleasant necessity is encountered. It must be confessed that the atmosphere of romance which lingers around this love-tale of the fair and sweet Ann Rutledge, so untimely taken away, is somewhat attenuated by the fact that only some fifteen months rolled by after she was laid in the ground before Lincoln was again intent upon matrimony. In the autumn of 1836 Miss Mary Owens, of Kentucky, appeared in New Salem,—a comely lass, with "large blue eyes," "fine trimmings," and a long and varied list of attractions. Lincoln immediately began to pay court to her, but in an ungainly and morbid fashion. It is impossible to avoid feeling that his mind was not yet in a natural and healthy condition. While offering to marry her, he advised her not to have him. Upon her part she found him "deficient in those little links which make up the chain of woman's happiness." So she would none of him, but wedded another and became the mother of some Confederate soldiers. Lincoln did not suffer on this second occasion as he had done on the first; and in the spring of 1838 he wrote upon the subject one of the most unfortunate epistles ever penned, in which he turned the whole affair into coarse and almost ribald ridicule. In fact he seems as much out of place in dealing with women and with love as he was in place in dealing with politicians and with politics, and it is pleasant to return from the former to the latter topics.

The spring of 1836 found Lincoln again nominating himself before the citizens of Sangamon County, but for the last time. His party denounced the caucus system as a "Yankee contrivance, intended to abridge the liberties of the people;" but they soon found that it would be as sensible to do battle with pikes and bows, after the invention of muskets and cannon, as to continue to oppose free self-nomination to the Jacksonian method of nomination by convention. In enjoying this last opportunity, not only of presenting himself, but also of constructing his own "platform," Lincoln published the following card:—

New Salem, June 13, 1836.

To The Editor of the Journal:—

In your paper of last Saturday I see a communication over the signature of "Many Voters" in which the candidates who are announced in the "Journal" are called upon to "show their hands." Agreed. Here's mine.

I go for all sharing the privileges of the government who assist in bearing its burdens. Consequently, I go for admitting all whites to the right of suffrage who pay taxes or bear arms (by no means excluding females).

If elected, I shall consider the whole people of Sangamon my constituents, as well those that oppose as those that support me.

While acting as their representative, I shall be governed by their will on all subjects upon which I have the means of knowing what their will is; and upon all others I shall do what my own judgment teaches me will best advance their interests. Whether elected or not, I go for distributing the proceeds of the sales of public lands to the several States to enable our State, in common with others, to dig canals and construct railroads without borrowing money and paying the interest on it.

If alive on the first Monday in November, I shall vote for Hugh L. White for President.

Very respectfully,   A. Lincoln.

The canvass was conducted after the usual fashion, with stump-speaking, fighting, and drinking. Western voters especially fancied the joint debate between rivals, and on such exciting occasions were apt to come to the arbitrament of fists and knives. But it is pleasant to hear that Lincoln calmed rather than excited such affrays, and that once, when Ninian W. Edwards climbed upon a table and screamed at his opponent the lie direct, Lincoln replied by "so fair a speech" that it quelled the discord. Henceforward he practiced a calm, carefully-weighed, dispassionate style in presenting facts and arguments. Even if he cultivated it from appreciation of its efficiency, at least his skill in it was due to the fact that it was congenial to his nature, and that his mind worked instinctively along these lines. His mental constitution, his way of thinking, were so honest that he always seemed to be a man sincerely engaged in seeking the truth, and who, when he believed that he had found it, would tell it precisely as he saw it, and tell it all. This was the distinguishing trait or habit which differentiates Lincoln from too many other political speakers and writers in the country. Yet with it he combined the character of a practical politician and a stanch party man. No party has a monopoly of truth and is always in the right; but Lincoln, with the advantage of being naturally fair-minded to a rare degree, understood that the best ingenuity is fairness, and that the second best ingenuity is the appearance of fairness.

He was absurdly misplaced as a member of the Committee on Finance. Never in his life did he show the slightest measure of "money sense."

A pleasant touch of his humor illumined this campaign. George Forquer, once a Whig but now a Democrat and an office-holder, had lately built for himself the finest house in Springfield, and had decorated it with the first lightning-rod ever seen in the neighborhood. One day, after Forquer had been berating Lincoln as a young man who must "be taken down," Lincoln turned to the audience with a few words: "It is for you, not for me, to say whether I am up or down. The gentleman has alluded to my being a young man; I am older in years than I am in the tricks and trades of politicians. I desire to live, and I desire place and distinction as a politician; but I would rather die now than, like the gentleman, live to see the day when I should have to erect a lightning-rod to protect a guilty conscience from an offended God."

He had declared his purpose to be governed by the will of his constituents in all matters in which he knew that will, and at this time he apparently held the American theory that the multitude probably possesses the highest wisdom, and that at any rate the majority is entitled to have its way.

There are other stories of this campaign, amusing and characteristic of the region and the times, but which there is not room to repeat. The result of it was that Sangamon County, hitherto Democratic, was now won by the Whigs, and that Lincoln had the personal satisfaction of leading the poll. The county had in the legislature nine representatives, tall fellows all, not one of them standing less than six feet, so that they were nicknamed "the Long Nine." Such was their authority that one of them afterward said: "All the bad or objectionable laws passed at that session of the legislature, and for many years afterward, were chargeable to the management and influence of 'the Long Nine.'" This was a damning confession, for the "bad and objectionable" laws of that session were numerous. A mania possessed the people. The whole State was being cut up into towns and cities and house-lots, so that town-lots were said to be the only article of export. A system of internal improvements at the public expense was pushed forward with incredible recklessness. The State was to be "gridironed" with thirteen hundred miles of railroad; the courses of the rivers were to be straightened; and where nature had neglected to supply rivers, canals were to be dug. A loan of twelve millions of dollars was authorized, and the counties not benefited thereby received gifts of cash. The bonds were issued and sent to the bankers of New York and of Europe, and work was vigorously begun. The terrible financial panic of 1837 ought to have administered an early check to this madness. But it did not. Resolutions of popular conventions instructed legislators to institute "a general system of internal improvements," which should be "commensurate with the wants of the people;" and the lawgivers obeyed as implicitly as if each delegate was lighting his steps by an Aladdin's lamp.

With this mad current Lincoln swam as wildly and as ignorantly as did any of his comrades. He was absurdly misplaced as a member of the Committee on Finance. Never in his life did he show the slightest measure of "money sense." He had, however, declared his purpose to be governed by the will of his constituents in all matters in which he knew that will, and at this time he apparently held the American theory that the multitude probably possesses the highest wisdom, and that at any rate the majority is entitled to have its way. Therefore, in this ambitious enterprise of putting Illinois at the very forefront of the civilized world by an outburst of fine American energy, his ardor was as warm as that of the warmest, and his intelligence was as utterly misled as that of the most ignorant. He declared his ambition to be "the DeWitt Clinton of Illinois." After the inevitable crash had come, amid the perplexity of general ruin and distress, he honestly acknowledged that he had blundered very badly. Nevertheless, no vengeance was exacted of him by the people; which led Governor Ford to say that it is safer for a politician to be wrong with his constituents than to be right against them, and to illustrate this profound truth by naming Lincoln among the "spared monuments of popular wrath."

"The Long Nine" had in this legislature a task peculiarly their own: to divide Sangamon County, and to make Springfield instead of Vandalia the state capital. Amid all the whirl of the legislation concerning improvements Lincoln kept this especial purpose always in view. It is said that his skill was infinite, and that he never lost heart. He gained the reputation of being the best "log-roller" in the legislature, and no measure got the support of the "Long Nine" without a contract for votes to be given in return for the removal of the state capital. It is unfortunate that such methods should enjoy the prestige of having been conspicuously practiced by Abraham Lincoln, but the evidence seems to establish the fact. That there was anything objectionable in the skillful performance of such common transactions as the trading of votes probably never occurred to him, being a professional politician, any more than it did to his constituents, who triumphed noisily in this success, and welcomed their candidates home with great popular demonstrations of approval.

The thunderous declamatory style was then regarded in the West as the only true eloquence. He learned better, in course of time, and so did the West.

A more agreeable occurrence at this session is the position taken by Lincoln concerning slavery, a position which was looked upon with extreme disfavor in those days in that State, and which he voluntarily assumed when he was not called upon to act or commit himself in any way concerning the matter. During the session sundry resolutions were passed, disapproving abolition societies and doctrines, asserting the sacredness of the right of property in slaves in the slave States, and alleging that it would be against good faith to abolish slavery in the District of Columbia without the consent of the citizens of the District. Two days before the end of the session, March 3, 1837, Lincoln introduced a strenuous protest. It bore only one signature besides his own, and doubtless this fact was fortunate for Lincoln, since it probably prevented the document from attracting the attention and resentment of a community which, at the time, by no means held the opinion that there was either "injustice" or "bad policy" in the great "institution" of the South. It was within a few months after this very time that the atrocious persecution and murder of Lovejoy took place in the neighboring town of Alton.

In such hours as he could snatch from politics and bread-winning Lincoln had continued to study law, and in March, 1837, he was admitted to the bar. He decided to establish himself in Springfield, where certainly he deserved a kindly welcome in return for what he had done towards making it the capital. It was a little town of only between one and two thousand inhabitants, but to Lincoln it seemed a metropolis. "There is a great deal of flourishing about in carriages here," he wrote; there were also social distinctions, and real aristocrats, who wore ruffled shirts, and even adventured "fair top-boots" in the "unfathomable" mud of streets which knew neither sidewalks nor pavements.

Now and again, in these early days, when his horizon could hardly have ranged beyond the state legislature and the lower house of Congress, he uttered some sentences which betrayed longings of a high moral grade, and indicated that office and power were already regarded by him as the opportunities for great actions.

Lincoln came into the place bringing all his worldly belongings in a pair of saddle-bags. He found there John T. Stuart, his comrade in the Black Hawk campaign, engaged in the practice of the law. The two promptly arranged a partnership. But Stuart was immersed in that too common mixture of law and politics in which the former jealous mistress is apt to take the traditional revenge upon her half-hearted suitor. Such happened in this case; and these two partners, both making the same blunder of yielding imperfect allegiance to their profession, paid the inevitable penalty; they got perhaps work enough in mere point of quantity, but it was neither interesting nor lucrative. Such business, during the four years which he passed with Stuart, did not wean Lincoln from his natural fondness for matters political. At the same time he was a member of sundry literary gatherings and debating societies. Such of his work as has been preserved does not transcend the ordinary productions of a young man trying his wings in clumsy flights of oratory; but he had the excuse that the thunderous declamatory style was then regarded in the West as the only true eloquence. He learned better, in course of time, and so did the West; and it was really good fortune that he passed through the hobbledehoy period in the presence of audiences whose taste was no better than his own.

Occasionally amid the tedium of these high-flown commonplaces there opens a fissure through which the inner spirit of the man looks out for an instant. It is well known that Lincoln was politically ambitious; his friends knew it, his biographers have said it, he himself avowed it. Now and again, in these early days, when his horizon could hardly have ranged beyond the state legislature and the lower house of Congress, he uttered some sentences which betrayed longings of a high moral grade, and indicated that office and power were already regarded by him as the opportunities for great actions. Strenuous as ought to be the objection to that tone in speaking of Lincoln which seems to proceed from beneath the sounding-board of the pulpit, and which uses him as a Sunday-school figure to edify a piously admiring world, yet it certainly seems a plain fact that his day-dreams at this period foreshadowed the acts of his later years, and that what he pleased himself with imagining was not the acquirement of official position but the achievement of some great benefit for mankind. He did not, of course, expect to do this as a philanthropist; for he understood himself sufficiently to know that his road lay in the public service. Accordingly he talks not as Clarkson or Wilberforce, but as a public man, of "emancipating slaves," of eliminating slavery and drunkenness from the land; at the same time he speaks thus not as a politician shrewdly anticipating the coming popular impulse, but as one desiring to stir that impulse. When he said, in his manifesto in 1832, that he had "no other ambition so great as that of being truly esteemed by his fellow-men," he uttered words which in the mouths of most politicians have the irritating effect of the dreariest and cheapest of platitudes; but he obviously uttered them with the sincerity of a deep inward ambition, that kind of an ambition which is often kept sacred from one's nearest intimates. Many side glimpses show him in this light, and it seems to be the genuine and uncolored one.

In 1838 Lincoln was again elected a member of the lower house of the legislature, and many are the amusing stories told of the canvass. It was in this year that he made sudden onslaught on the demagogue Dick Taylor, and opening with a sudden jerk the artful colonel's waistcoat, displayed a glittering wealth of jewelry hidden temporarily beneath it. There is also the tale of his friend Baker haranguing a crowd in the store beneath Lincoln's office. The audience differed with Baker, and was about to punish him severely for the difference, when Lincoln dangled down through a trap-door in the ceiling, intimated his intention to share in the fight if there was to be one, and brought the audience to a more pacific frame of mind. Such amenities of political debate at least tested some of the qualities of the individual. The Whig party made him their candidate for the speakership and he came within one vote of being elected. He was again a member of the Finance Committee; but financiering by those wise lawgivers was no longer so lightsome and exuberant a task as it had been. The hour of reckoning had come; and the business proved to be chiefly a series of humiliating and futile efforts to undo the follies of the preceding two and a half years. Lincoln shared in this disagreeable labor, as he had shared in the mania which had made it necessary. He admitted that he was "no financier," and gave evidence of the fact by submitting a bill which did not deserve to be passed, and was not. It can, however, be said for him that he never favored repudiation, as some of his comrades did.

Of Lincoln's [1840] speeches only one has been preserved, and it leads to the conclusion that nothing of value was lost when the others perished.

In 1840 Lincoln was again elected, again was the nominee of the Whig party for the speakership, and again was beaten by Ewing, the Democratic candidate, who mustered 46 votes against 36 for Lincoln. This legislature held only one session, and apparently Holland's statement, that "no important business of general interest was transacted," is a fair summary. Lincoln did only one memorable thing, and that unfortunately was discreditable. In a close and exciting contest, he, with two other Whigs, jumped out of the window in order to break a quorum. It is gratifying to hear from the chronicler of the event, who was one of the parties concerned, that "Mr. Lincoln always regretted that he entered into that arrangement, as he deprecated everything that savored of the revolutionary."

The year 1840 was made lively throughout the country by the spirited and rollicking campaign which the Whigs made on behalf of General Harrison. In that famous struggle for "Tippecanoe and Tyler too," the log cabin, hard cider, and the 'coon skin were the popular emblems which seemed to lend picturesqueness and enthusiasm and a kind of Western spirit to the electioneering everywhere in the land. In Illinois Lincoln was a candidate on the Whig electoral ticket, and threw himself with great zeal into the congenial task of "stumping" the State. Douglas was doing the same duty on the other side, and the two had many encounters. Of Lincoln's speeches only one has been preserved, and it leads to the conclusion that nothing of value was lost when the others perished. The effusion was in the worst style of the effervescent and exuberant school of that region and generation. Nevertheless, it may have had the greatest merit which oratory can possess, in being perfectly adapted to the audience to which it was addressed. But rhetoric could not carry Illinois for the Whigs; the Democrats cast the vote of the State.

CHAPTER III

LOVE; A DUEL; LAW, AND CONGRESS

United States Capitol

"Now, if you should hear any one say that Lincoln don't want to go to Congress,… he is mistaken."

Collaterally with law and politics, Lincoln was at this time engaged with that almost grotesque courtship which led to his marriage. The story is a long and strange one; in its best gloss it is not agreeable, and in its worst version it is exceedingly disagreeable. In any form it is inexplicable, save so far as the apparent fact that his mind was somewhat disordered can be taken as an explanation. In 1839 Miss Mary Todd, who had been born in Lexington, Kentucky, December 13, 1818, came to Springfield to stay with her sister, Mrs. Ninian W. Edwards. The Western biographers describe her as "gifted with rare talents," as "high-bred, proud, brilliant, witty," as "aristocratic" and "accomplished," and as coming from a "long and distinguished ancestral line." Later in her career critics with more exacting standards gave other descriptions. There is, however, no doubt that in point of social position and acquirements she stood at this time much above Lincoln.

Upon Lincoln's part it was a peculiar wooing, a series of morbid misgivings as to the force of his affection, of alternate ardor and coldness, advances and withdrawals, and every variety of strange language and freakish behavior. In the course of it, oddly enough, his omnipresent competitor, Douglas, crossed his path, his rival in love as well as in politics, and ultimately outstripped by him in each alike. After many months of this queer, uncertain zigzag progress, it was arranged that the marriage should take place on January 1, 1841. At the appointed hour the company gathered, the supper was set out, and the bride, "bedecked in veil and silken gown, and nervously toying with the flowers in her hair," according to the graphic description of Mr. Herndon, sat in her sister's house awaiting the coming of her lover. She waited, but he came not, and soon his friends were searching the town for him. Towards morning they found him. Some said that he was insane; if he was not, he was at least suffering from such a terrible access of his constitutional gloom that for some time to come it was considered necessary to watch him closely. His friend Speed took him away upon a long visit to Kentucky, from which he returned in a much improved mental condition, but soon again came under the influence of Miss Todd's attractions.

The memory of the absurd result of the recent effort at marriage naturally led to the avoidance of publicity concerning the second undertaking. So nothing was said till the last moment; then the license was procured, a few friends were hastily notified, and the ceremony was performed, all within a few hours, on November 4, 1842. A courtship marked by so many singularities was inevitably prolific of gossip; and by all this tittle-tattle, in which it is absolutely impossible to separate probably a little truth from much fiction, the bride suffered more than the groom. Among other things it was asserted that Lincoln at last came to the altar most reluctantly. One says that he was "pale and trembling, as if being driven to slaughter;" another relates that the little son of a friend, noticing that his toilet had been more carefully made than usual, asked him where he was going, and that he gloomily responded: "To hell, I suppose." Probably enough, however, these anecdotes are apocryphal; for why the proud and high-tempered Miss Todd should have held so fast to an unwilling lover, who had behaved so strangely and seemed to offer her so little, is a conundrum which has been answered by no better explanation than the very lame one, that she

That there were better and greater lawyers than he is unquestionable; that he was primarily a politician and only secondarily a lawyer is equally beyond denial.

foresaw his future distinction. It was her misfortune that she failed to make herself popular, so that no one has cared in how disagreeable or foolish a position any story places her. She was charged with having a sharp tongue, a sarcastic wit, and a shrewish temper, over which perilous traits she had no control. It is related that her sister, Mrs. Edwards, opposed the match, from a belief that the two were utterly uncongenial, and later on this came to be the accepted belief of the people at large. That Mrs. Lincoln often severely harassed her husband always has been and always will be believed. One would gladly leave the whole topic veiled in that privacy which ought always to be accorded to domestic relations which are supposed to be only imperfectly happy; but his countrymen have not shown any such respect to Mr. Lincoln, and it no longer is possible wholly to omit mention of a matter about which so much has been said and written. Moreover, it has usually been supposed that the influence of

Mrs Lincoln upon her husband was unceasing and powerful, and that her moods and her words constituted a very important element in his life.

Another disagreeable incident of this period was the quarrel with James A. Shields. In the summer of 1842 sundry coarse assaults upon Shields, attributed in great part, or wholly, to the so-called trenchant and witty pen of Miss Todd, appeared in the Springfield "Journal." Lincoln accepted the responsibility for them, received and reluctantly accepted a challenge, and selected broadswords as the weapons! "Friends," however, brought about an "explanation," and the conflict was avoided. But ink flowed in place of blood, and the newspapers were filled with a mass of silly, grandiloquent, blustering, insolent, and altogether pitiable stuff. All the parties concerned were placed in a most humiliating light, and it is gratifying to hear that Lincoln had at least the good feeling to be heartily ashamed of the affair, so that he "always seemed willing to forget" it. But every veil which he ever sought to throw over anything concerning himself has had the effect of an irresistible provocation to drag the subject into the strongest glare of publicity.

All the while, amid so many distractions, Lincoln was seeking a livelihood at the bar. On April 14, 1841, a good step was taken by dissolving the partnership with Stuart and the establishment of a new partnership with Stephen T. Logan, lately judge of the Circuit Court of the United States, and whom Arnold calls "the head of the bar at the capital." This gentleman, though not averse to politics, was a close student, assiduous in his attention to business, and very accurate and methodical in his ways. Thus he furnished a shining example of precisely the qualities which Lincoln had most need to cultivate, and his influence upon Lincoln was marked and beneficial. They continued together until September 20, 1843, when they separated, and on the same day Lincoln, heretofore a junior, became the senior in a new partnership with William H. Herndon. This firm was never formally dissolved up to the day of Lincoln's death.

When Lincoln was admitted to the bar the practice of the law was in a very crude condition in Illinois. General principles gathered from a few text-books formed the simple basis upon which lawyers tried cases and framed arguments in improvised court-rooms. But the advance was rapid and carried Lincoln forward with it. The raw material, if the phrase may be pardoned, was excellent; there were many men in the State who united a natural aptitude for the profession with high ability, ambition, and a progressive spirit. Lincoln was brought in contact with them all, whether they rode his circuit or not, because the federal courts were held only in Springfield. Among them were Stephen A. Douglas, Lyman Trumbull, afterward for a long while chairman of the Judiciary Committee of the national Senate, David Davis, afterward a senator, and an associate justice of the Supreme Court of the United States; O. H. Browning, Ninian W. Edwards, Edward D. Baker, Justin Butterfield, Judge Logan, and more. Precisely what position Lincoln occupied among these men it is difficult to say with accuracy, because it is impossible to know just how much of the praise which has been bestowed upon him is the language of eulogy or of the brotherly courtesy of the bar, and how much is a discriminating valuation of his qualities. That in the foregoing list there were better and greater lawyers than he is unquestionable; that he was primarily a politician and only secondarily a lawyer is equally beyond denial. He has been described also as "a case lawyer," that is to say, a lawyer who studies each case as it comes to him simply by and for itself, a method which makes the practitioner rather than the jurist. That Lincoln was ever learned in the science is hardly pretended. In fact it was not possible that the divided allegiance which he gave to his profession for a score of years could have achieved such a result. But it is said, and the well-known manner of his mental operations makes it easy to believe, that his arguments had a marvelous simplicity and clearness, alike in thought and in expression. To these traits they owed their great force; and a legal argument can have no higher traits; fine-drawn subtlety is undeniably an inferior quality. Noteworthy above all else was his extraordinary capacity for statement; all agree that his statement of his case and his presentation of the facts and the evidence were so plain and fair as to be far more convincing than the argument which was built upon them. Again it may be said that the power to state in this manner is as high in the order of intellectual achievement as anything within forensic possibilities.

As an advocate Lincoln seems to have ranked better than he did in the discussion of pure points of law. When he warmed to his work his power over the emotions of a jury was very great. A less dignified but not less valuable capacity lay in his humor and his store of illustrative anecdotes. But the one trait, which all agree in attributing to him and which above all others will redound to his honor, at least in the mind of the layman, is that he was only efficient when his client was in the right, and that he made but indifferent work in a wrong cause. He was preëminently the honest lawyer, the counsel fitted to serve the litigant who was justly entitled to win. His power of lucid statement was of little service when the real facts were against him; and his eloquence seemed paralyzed when he did not believe thoroughly that his client had a just cause. He generally refused to take cases unless he could see that as matter of genuine right he ought to win them. People who consulted him were at times bluntly advised to withdraw from an unjust or a hard-hearted contention, or were bidden to seek other counsel. He could even go the length of leaving a case, while actually conducting it, if he became satisfied of unfairness on the part of his client; and when a coadjutor won a case from which he had withdrawn *in transitu*, so to speak, he refused to accept any portion of the fee. Such habits may not meet with the same measure of commendation from professional men which they will command on the part of others; but those who are not members of this ingenious profession, contemning the fine logic which they fail to overcome, stubbornly insist upon admiring the lawyer who refuses to subordinate right to law. In this respect Lincoln accepted the ideals of laymen rather than the doctrines of his profession.

In the presidential campaign of 1844, in which Henry Clay was the candidate of the Whig party, Lincoln was nominated upon the Whig electoral ticket. He was an ardent admirer of Clay and he threw himself into this contest with great zeal. Oblivious of courts and clients, he devoted himself to "stumping" Illinois and a part of Indiana. When Illinois sent nine Democratic electors to vote for James K. Polk, his disappointment was bitter. All the members of the defeated party had a peculiar sense of personal chagrin upon this occasion, and Lincoln felt it even more than others. It is said that two years later a visit to Ashland resulted in a disillusionment, and that his idol then came down from its pedestal, or at least the pedestal was made much lower.

In March, 1843, Lincoln had hopes that the Whigs would nominate him as their candidate for the national House of Representatives. In the canvass he developed some strength, but not quite enough, and the result was somewhat ludicrous, for Sangamon County made him a delegate to the nominating convention with instructions to vote for one of his own competitors, Colonel Edward D. Baker, the gallant gentleman and brilliant orator who fell at Ball's Bluff. The prize was finally carried off by Colonel John J. Hardin, who afterward died at Buena Vista. By a change of election periods the next convention was held in 1844, and this time Lincoln publicly declined to make a contest for the nomination against Colonel Baker, who accordingly received it and was elected. It has been said that an agreement was made between Hardin, Baker, Lincoln, and Judge Logan, whereby each should be allowed one term in Congress, without competition on the part of any of the others; but the story

It was not a very great or remarkable speech, but it was a good one; he spoke sensibly, clearly, and with precision of thought; he sought his strength in the facts; his best intellectual qualities were plainly visible. The resolutions were not acted upon, and doubtless their actual passage had never been expected; but they were a good shot well placed.

does not seem altogether trustworthy, nor wholly corroborated by the facts. Possibly there may have been a courteous understanding between them. It has, however, been spoken of as a very reprehensible bargain, and Lincoln has been zealously defended against the reproach of having entered into it. Why, if indeed it ever was made, it had this objectionable complexion is a point in the inscrutable moralities of politics which is not plain to those uninitiated in these ethical mysteries.

In the year 1846 Lincoln again renewed his pursuit of the coveted honor, as Holland very properly puts it. Nothing is more absurd than statements to the purport that he was "induced to accept" the nomination, statements which he himself would have heard with honest laughter. Only three years ago he had frankly written to a friend: "Now, if you should hear any one say that Lincoln don't want to go to Congress, I wish you, as a personal friend of mine, would tell him you have reason to believe he is mistaken. The truth is I would [should] like to go very much." Now, the opportunity being at hand, he spared no pains to compass it. In spite of the alleged agreement Hardin made reconnoissances in the district, which Lincoln met with counter-manifestations so vigorous that on February 26 Hardin withdrew, and on May 1 Lincoln was nominated. Against him the Democrats set Peter Cartwright, the famous itinerant preacher of the Methodists, whose strenuous and popular eloquence had rung in the ears of every Western settler. Stalwart, aggressive, possessing all the qualities adapted to win the good-will of such a constituency, the Apostle of the West was a dangerous antagonist. But Lincoln had political capacity in a rare degree. Foresight and insight, activity and the power to organize and to direct, were his. In this campaign his eye was upon every one; individuals, newspaper editors, political clubs, got their inspiration and their guidance from him. Such thoroughness deserved and achieved an extraordinary success; and at the polls, in August, the district gave him a majority of 1,511. In the latest presidential campaign it had given Clay a majority of 914; and two years later it gave Taylor a majority of 1,501. Sangamon County gave Lincoln a majority of 690, the largest given to any candidate from 1836 to 1850, inclusive. Moreover, Lincoln was the only Whig who secured a place in the Illinois delegation.

Though elected in the summer of 1846, it was not until December 6, 1847, that the Thirtieth Congress began its first session. Robert C. Winthrop was chosen speaker of the House, by 110 votes out of 218. The change in the political condition was marked; in the previous House the Democrats had numbered 142 and the Whigs only 75; in this House the Whigs were 116, the Democrats 108. Among the members were John Quincy Adams, Andrew Johnson, Alexander H. Stephens, Howell Cobb, David Wilmot, Jacob Collamer, Robert Toombs, with many more scarcely less familiar names. The Mexican war was drawing towards its close, and most of the talking in Congress had relation to it. The whole Whig party denounced it at the time, and the nation has been more than half ashamed of it ever since. By adroit manoeuvres Polk had forced the fight upon a weak and reluctant nation, and had made to his own people false statements as to both the facts and the merits of the quarrel. The rebuke which they had now administered, by changing the large Democratic majority into a minority, "deserves," says von Holst, "to be counted among the most meritorious proofs of the sound and honorable feeling of the American nation." But while the administration had thus smirched the inception and the whole character of the war with meanness and dishonor, the generals and the army were winning abundant glory for the national arms. Good strategy achieved a series of brilliant victories, and fortunately for the Whigs General Taylor and General Scott, together with a large proportion of the most distinguished regimental officers, were of their party. This aided them essentially in their policy, which was, to denounce the entering into the war but to vote all necessary supplies for its vigorous prosecution.

Into this scheme of his party Lincoln entered with hearty concurrence. A week after the House met he closed a letter to his partner with the remark: "As you are all so anxious for me to distinguish myself, I have concluded to do so before long," and what he said humorously he probably meant seriously. Accordingly he soon afterward introduced a series of resolutions, which, under the nickname of "The Spot Resolutions," attracted some attention. Quoting in his preamble sundry paragraphs of the President's message of May 11, 1846, to the purport that Mexico had "invaded *our territory*," and had "shed the blood of our citizens *on our own soil*," he then requested the President to state *"the spot"* where these and other alleged occurrences had taken place. His first "little speech" was on "a post-office question of no general interest;" and he found himself "about as badly scared and no worse" than when he spoke in court. So a little later, January 12, 1848, he ventured to call up his resolutions and to make an elaborate speech upon them. It was not a very great or remarkable speech, but it was a good one, and not conceived in the fervid and florid style which defaced his youthful efforts; he spoke sensibly, clearly, and with precision of thought; he sought his strength in the facts, and went in straight pursuit of the truth; his best intellectual qualities were plainly visible. The resolutions were not acted upon, and doubtless their actual passage had never been expected; but they were a good shot well placed; and they were sufficiently noteworthy to save Lincoln from being left among the herd of the noboodies of the House

In view of his future career, but for no other reason, a brief paragraph is worth quoting. He says:—

"Any people anywhere, being inclined and having the power, have the *right* to rise up and shake off the existing government, and form a new one that suits them better. This is a most valuable, a most sacred right,—a right which, we hope and believe, is to liberate the world. Nor is this right confined to cases in which the whole people of an existing government may choose to exercise it.

When his term of service in Congress was over, Lincoln was offered the governorship of the newly organized Territory of Oregon.

Any portion of such people, that *can*, may revolutionize, and make their *own* of so much of the territory as they inhabit." This doctrine, so comfortably applied to Texas in 1848, seemed unsuitable for the Confederate States in 1861. But possibly the point lay in the words, "having the power," and "can," for the Texans "had the power" and "could," and the South had it not and could not; and so Lincoln's practical proviso saved his theoretical consistency; though he must still have explained how either Texas or the South could know whether they "had the power," and "could," except by trial.

Lincoln's course concerning the war and the administration did not please his constituents. With most of the Whigs he voted for Ashmun's amendment, which declared that the war had been "unnecessarily and unconstitutionally commenced by the President." But soon he heard that the people in Springfield were offended at a step which might weaken the administration in time of stress; and even if the President had transcended the Constitution, they preferred to deny rather than to admit the fact. When Douglas afterward charged Lincoln with lack of patriotism, Lincoln replied that he had not chosen to "skulk," and, feeling obliged to vote, he had voted for "the truth" rather than for "a lie." He remarked also that he, with the Whigs generally, always voted for the supply bills. He took and maintained his position with entire manliness and honesty, and stated his principles with perfect clearness, neither shading nor abating nor coloring by any conciliatory or politic phrase. It was a question of conscience, and he met it point-blank. Many of his critics remained dissatisfied, and it is believed that his course cost the next Whig candidate in the district votes which he could not afford to lose. It is true that another paid this penalty, yet Lincoln himself would have liked well to take his chance as the candidate. To those "who desire that I should be reëlected," he wrote to Herndon, "I can say, as Mr. Clay said of the annexation of Texas, that '*personally* I would not object.' ... If it should so happen *that nobody else wishes to be elected*, I could not refuse the people the right of sending me again. But to enter myself as a competitor of others, or to authorize any one so to enter me, is what my word and honor forbid." It did so happen that Judge Logan, whose turn it seemed to be, wished the nomination and received it. He was, however, defeated, and probably paid the price of Lincoln's scrupulous honesty.

In the canvassing of the spring of 1848 Lincoln was an ardent advocate for the nomination of General Taylor as the Whig candidate for the presidency; for he appreciated how much greater was the strength of the military hero, with all that could be said against him, than was that of Mr. Clay, whose destiny was so disappointingly non-presidential. When the nomination went according to his wishes, he entered into the campaign with as much zeal as his congressional duties would permit,—indeed, with somewhat an excess of zeal, for he delivered on the floor of the House an harangue in favor of the general which was little else than a stump speech, admirably adapted for a backwoods audience, but grossly out of place where it was spoken. He closed it with an assault on General Cass, as a military man, which was designed to be humorous, and has, therefore, been quoted with unfortunate frequency. So soon as Congress adjourned he was able to seek a more legitimate arena in New England, whither he went at once and delivered many speeches, none of which have been preserved.

Lincoln's position upon the slavery question in this Congress was that of moderate hostility. In the preceding Congress, the Twenty-ninth, the famous Wilmot Proviso, designed to exclude slavery from any territory which the United States should acquire from Mexico, had passed the House and had been killed in the Senate. In the Thirtieth Congress efforts to the same end were renewed in various forms, always with Lincoln's favor. He once said that he had voted for the principle of the Wilmot Proviso "about forty-two times," which, if not an accurate mathematical computation, was a vivid expression of his stanch adherence to the doctrine. At the second session Mr. Lincoln voted against a bill to prohibit the slave trade in the District of Columbia, because he did not approve its form; and then introduced another bill, which he himself had drawn. This prohibited bringing slaves into the District, except as household servants by government officials who were citizens of slave States; it also prohibited selling them to be taken away from the District; children born of slave mothers after January 1, 1850, were to be subject to temporary apprenticeship and finally to be made free; owners of slaves might collect from the government their full cash value as the price of their freedom; fugitive slaves escaping into Washington and Georgetown were to be returned; finally the measure was to be submitted to popular vote in the District. This was by no means a measure of abolitionist coloring, although Lincoln obtained for it the support of Joshua R. Giddings, who believed it "as good a bill as we could get at this time," and was "willing to pay for slaves in order to save them from the Southern market." It recognized the right of property in slaves, which the Abolitionists denied; also it might conceivably be practicable, a characteristic which rarely marked the measures of the Abolitionists, who professed to be pure moralists rather than practical politicians. From this first move to the latest which he made in this great business, Lincoln never once broke connection with practicability. On this occasion he had actually succeeded in obtaining from Mr. Seaton, editor of the "National Intelligencer" and mayor of Washington, a promise of support, which gave him a little prospect of success. Later, however, the Southern Congressmen drew this influential gentleman to their side, and thereby rendered the passage of the bill impossible; at the close of the session it lay with the other corpses in that grave called "the table."

When his term of service in Congress was over Lincoln sought, but failed to obtain, the position of Commissioner of the General Lands Office. He was offered the governorship of the newly organized Territory of Oregon; but this, controlled by the sensible advice of his wife, he fortunately declined.

CHAPTER IV
NORTH AND SOUTH

Springfield home

*"I regret my defeat moderately, but am
not nervous about it."*

The Ordinance of 1787 established that slavery should never exist in any part of that vast northwestern territory which had then lately been ceded by sundry States to the Confederation. This Ordinance could not be construed otherwise than as an integral part of the transaction of cession, and was forever unalterable, because it represented in a certain way a part of the consideration in a contract, and was also in the nature of a declaration of trust undertaken by the Congress of the Confederation with the granting States. The article "was agreed to without opposition;" but almost contemporaneously, in the sessions of that convention which framed the Constitution, debate waxed hot upon the topic which was then seen to present grave obstacles to union. It was true that many of the wisest Southerners of that generation regarded the institution as a menacing misfortune; they however could not ignore the fact that it was a "misfortune" of that peculiar kind which was endured with much complacency by those afflicted by it; and it was equally certain that the great body of slave-owners would resent any effort to relieve them of their burden. Hence there were placed in the Constitution provisions in behalf of slavery which involved an admission that the institution needed protection, and should receive it. The idea of protection implied the existence of hostility either of men or of circumstances, or of both. Thus by the Ordinance and the Constitution, taken together, there was already indirectly recognized an antagonism between the institutions, interests, and opinions of the South and those of the North.

Slowly this feeling of opposition grew. The first definite mark of the growth was the struggle over the admission of Missouri, in 1820. This was settled by the famous "Compromise," embodied in the Act of March 6, 1820, whereby the people of the Territory of Missouri were allowed to frame a state government with no restriction against slavery; but a clause also enacted that slavery should never be permitted in any part of the remainder of the public territory lying north of the parallel of 36° 30'. By its efficiency during thirty-four years of constantly increasing strain this legislation was proved to be a remarkable political achievement; and as the people saw it perform so long and so well a service so vital they came to regard it as only less sacred than the Constitution itself. Even Douglas, who afterward led in repealing it, declared that it had an "origin akin to the Constitution," and that it was "canonized in the hearts of the American people as a sacred thing." Yet during the long quietude which it brought, each section kept a jealous eye upon the other; and especially was the scrutiny of the South uneasy, for she saw ever more and more plainly the disturbing truth that her institution needed protection. Being in derogation of natural right, it was peculiarly dependent upon artificial sustention; the South would not express the condition in this language, but acted upon the idea none the less. It was true that the North was not aggressive towards slavery, but was observing it with much laxity and indifference; that the crusading spirit was sleeping soundly, and even the proselyting temper was feeble. But this state of Northern feeling could not relieve the South from the harassing consciousness that slavery needed not only toleration, but positive *protection* at the hands of a population whose institutions were naturally antagonistic to the slave idea. This being the case, she must be alarmed at seeing that population steadily outstripping her own in numbers and wealth.

*Such were the terms of an arrangement in which
every man saw so much which he himself disliked
that he felt sure that others must be satisfied.*

Since she could not possibly even hold this disproportion stationary, her best resource seemed to be to endeavor to keep it practically harmless by maintaining a balance of power in the government. Thus it became unwritten law that slave States and free States must be equal in number, so that the South could not be outvoted in the Senate. This system was practicable for a while, yet not a very long while; for the North was filling up that great northwestern region, which was eternally dedicated to freedom, and full-grown communities could not forever be kept outside the pale of statehood. On the other hand, apart from any question of numbers, the South could make no counter-expansion, because she lay against a foreign country. After a time, however, Texas opportunely rebelled against Mexico, and then the opportunity for removing this obstruction was too obvious and too tempting to be lost. A brief period of so-called independence on the part of Texas was followed by the annexation of her territory to the United States, with the proviso that from her great area might in the future be cut off still four other States. Slavery had been abolished in all Mexican territory, and Texas had been properly a "free" country; but in becoming a part of the United States she became also a slave State.

Mexico had declared that annexation of Texas would constitute a *casus belli*, yet she was wisely laggard in beginning vindictive hostilities against a power which could so easily whip her, and she probably never would have done so had the United States rested content with an honest boundary line. But this President Polk would not do, and by theft and falsehood he at last fairly drove the Mexicans into a war, in which they were so excessively beaten that the administration found itself able to gather more plunder than it had expected. By the treaty of peace the United States not only extended unjustly the southwestern boundary of Texas, but also got New Mexico and California. To forward this result, Polk had asked the House to place $2,000,000 at his disposal. Thereupon, as an amendment to the bill granting this sum, Wilmot introduced his famous proviso, prohibiting slavery in any part of the territory to be acquired. Repeatedly and in various shapes was the substance of this proviso voted upon, but always it was voted down. Though New Mexico had come out from under the rule of despised Mexico as "free" country, a contrary destiny was marked out for it in its American character. A plausible suggestion was made to extend the sacred line of the Missouri Compromise westward to the Pacific Ocean; and very little of the new country lay north of that line.

By all these transactions the South seemed to be scoring many telling points in its game. They were definite points, which all could see and estimate; yet a price, which was considerable, though less definite, less easy to see and to estimate, had in fact been paid for them; for the antagonism of the rich and teeming North to the Southern institution and to the Southern policy for protecting it had been spread and intensified to a degree which involved a menace fully offsetting the Southern territorial gain. One of the indications of this state of feeling was the organization of the "Free Soil" party.

Almost simultaneously with this important advancement of the Southern policy there occurred an event, operative upon the other side, which certainly no statesman could have foreseen. Gold was discovered in California, and in a few months a torrent of immigrants poured over the land. The establishment of an efficient government became a pressing need. In Congress they debated the matter hotly; the friends of the Wilmot proviso met in bitter conflict the advocates of the westward extension of the line of 36° 30'. Neither side could prevail, and amid intense excitement the Thirtieth Congress expired. For the politicians this was well enough, but for the Californians organization was such an instant necessity that they now had to help themselves to it. So they promptly elected a Constitutional Convention, which assembled on September 1, 1849, and adjourned on October 13. Though this body held fifteen delegates who were immigrants from slave States, yet it was unanimous in presenting a Constitution which prohibited slavery, and which was at once accepted by a popular vote of 12,066 yeas against 811 nays.

Great then was the consternation of the Southern leaders when Californian delegates appeared immediately upon the assembling of the Thirty-first Congress, and asked for admission beneath this unlooked-for "free" charter of statehood. The shock was aggravated by the fact that New Mexico, actually instigated thereto by the slaveholding President Taylor himself, was likely to follow close in the Californian foot-tracks. The admission of Texas had for a moment disturbed the senatorial equilibrium between North and South, which, however, had quickly been restored by the admission of Wisconsin. But the South had nothing to offer to counterbalance California and New Mexico, which were being suddenly filched from her confident expectation. In this emergency those extremists in the South who offset the Abolitionists at the North fell back upon the appalling threat of disunion, which could hardly be regarded as an idle extravagance of the "hotspurs," since it was substantially certain that the Senate would never admit California with her anti-slavery Constitution; and thus a real crisis seemed at hand. Other questions also were cast into the seething caldron. Texas, whose boundaries were as uncertain as the ethics of politicians, set up a claim which included nearly all New Mexico, and so would have settled the question of slavery for that region at least. Further, the South called for a Fugitive Slave Law sufficiently stringent to be serviceable. Also, in encountering the Wilmot proviso, Southern statesmen had asserted the doctrine, far reaching and subversive of established ideas and of enacted laws, that Congress could not constitutionally interfere with the property-rights of citizens of the United States in the Territories, and that slaves were property. Amid such a confused and violent hurly-burly the perplexed body of order-loving citizens were, with reason, seriously alarmed.

To the great relief of these people and to the equal disgust of the extremist politicians, Henry Clay, the "great compromiser," was now announced to appear once more in the rôle which all felt that he alone could play. He came with much dramatic effect; an aged and broken man, he emerged from the retirement in which he seemed to have sought a brief rest before death should lay him low, and it was with an impressive air of sadness and of earnestness that

Lincoln recognized the futility of this whole arrangement, and said truly that the slavery question could "never be successfully compromised." Yet he accepted the situation, with the purpose of making of it the best that was possible.

he devoted the last remnants of his failing strength to save a country which he had served so long. His friends feared that he might not survive even a few months to reach the end of his patriotic task. On January 29, 1850, he laid before the Senate his "comprehensive scheme of adjustment." But it came not as oil upon the angry waters; every one was offended by one or another part of it, and at once there opened a war of debate which is among the most noteworthy and momentous in American history. Great men who belonged to the past and great men who were to belong to the future shared in the exciting controversies, which were prolonged over a period of more than half a year. Clay was constantly on his feet, doing battle with a voice which gained rather than lost force from its pathetic feebleness. "I am here," he solemnly said, "expecting soon to go hence, and owing no responsibility but to my own conscience and to God." Jefferson Davis spoke for the extension westward of the Missouri

Compromise line to the Pacific Ocean, with a proviso positively establishing slavery south of that line. Calhoun, from the edge of the grave, into which only a few weeks later he was to fall, once more faced his old adversaries. On March 4 he sat beside Mason of Virginia, while that gentleman read for him to a hushed audience the speech which he himself was too weak to deliver. Three days later Webster uttered that speech which made the seventh day of March almost as famous in the history of the United States as the Ides of the same month had been in that of Rome. In the eyes of the anti-slavery men of New England the fall of Webster was hardly less momentous than the fall of Caesar had appeared in the Eternal City. Seward also spoke a noteworthy speech, bringing upon himself infinite abuse by his bold phrase, *a higher law than the Constitution*. Salmon P. Chase followed upon the same side, in an exalted and prophetic strain. In that momentous session every man gave out what he felt to be his best, while anxious and excited millions devoured every word which the newspapers reported to them.

Clay had imprudently gathered the several matters of his Compromise into one bill, which was soon sneeringly nicknamed "the Omnibus Bill." It was sorely harassed by amendments, and when at last, on July 31, the Omnibus reached the end of its journey, it contained only one passenger, viz., a territorial government for Utah. Its trip had apparently ended in utter failure. But a careful study of individual proclivities showed that not improbably those measures might be passed one by one which could not be passed in combination. In this hope, five several bills, being all the ejected contents of the Omnibus, were brought forward, and each in turn had the success which had been denied to them together. First: Texas received $10,000,000, and for this price magnanimously relinquished her unfounded claim upon New Mexico. Second: California was admitted as a free State. Third: New Mexico was organized as a Territory, with the proviso that when she should form a state constitution the slavery question should be determined by the people, and that during her territorial existence the question of property in a slave should be left undisturbed by congressional action, to be determined by the Supreme Court of the United States. Fourth: A more efficient Fugitive Slave Law was passed. Fifth: Slave trading in the District of Columbia was abolished. Such were the terms of an arrangement in which every man saw so much which he himself disliked that he felt sure that others must be satisfied. Each plumed himself on his liberality in his concessions nobly made in behalf of public harmony. "The broad basis," says von Holst, "on which the compromise of 1850 rested, was the conviction of the great majority of the people, both North and South, that it was fair, reasonable, and patriotic to come to a friendly understanding."

Thus in the midsummer of 1850 did the nation, with intense relief, see the imminent disaster of civil discord averted,—or was it only postponed? It was ominous that no men who were deeply in earnest in public affairs were sincerely satisfied. The South saw no gain which offset the destruction of the balance of power by the admission of California. Thinking men at the North were alarmed at the recognition of the principle of non-intervention by Congress concerning slavery in the Territories, a principle which soon, under the seductive title of "popular sovereignty" in the Territories, threatened even that partial restriction heretofore given by the Missouri Compromise. Neither party felt sufficiently secure of the strength of its legal position to be altogether pleased at seeing the doctrine of treating the slave in the Territories as "property" cast into the lottery of the Supreme Court. Lincoln recognized the futility of this whole arrangement, and said truly that the slavery question could "never be successfully compromised." Yet he accepted the situation, with the purpose of making of it the best that was possible. The mass of the people, less far-sighted, were highly gratified at the passing of the great danger; refused to recognize that a more temporary compromise was never patched up to serve a turn; and applauded it so zealously that in preparing for the presidential campaign of 1852 each party felt compelled to declare emphatically—what all wise politicians knew to be false—the "finality" of the great Compromise of 1850. Never, never more was there to be a revival of the slavery agitation! Yet, at the same time, it was instinctively felt that the concord would cease at once if the nation should not give to the South a Democratic President! In this campaign Lincoln made a few speeches in Illinois in favor of Scott; but Herndon says that they were not very satisfactory efforts. Franklin Pierce was chosen, and slavery could have had no better man.

This doctrine of non-intervention by Congress with slavery in the Territories lay as the seed of mortal disease imbedded in the vitals of the great Compromise even at the hour of its birth. All the howlings of the political medicine-men in the halls of Congress, and in the wigwams where the party platforms were manufactured, could not defer the inevitable dissolution. The rapid peopling of the Pacific coast already made it imperative to provide some sort of governmental organization for the sparsely inhabited regions lying between these new lands and the fringe of population near the Mississippi. Accordingly bills were introduced to establish as a Territory the region which was afterward divided between Kansas and Nebraska; but at two successive sessions they failed to pass, more, as it seemed, from lack of interest than from any open hostility. In the course of debate it was explained, and not contradicted, that slavery was not mentioned in the bills because the Missouri

All the howlings of the political medicine-men in the halls of Congress could not defer the inevitable dissolution.

Compromise controlled that matter. Yet it was well known that the Missouri Compromise was no longer a sure barrier; for one wing of the pro-slavery party asserted that it was unconstitutional on the ground that slaves, being property, could not be touched in the Territories by congressional enactments; while another wing of the party preferred the plausible cry of "popular sovereignty," than which no words could ring truer in American ears; and no one doubted that, in order to give that sovereignty full sway, they would at any convenient moment vote to repeal even the "sacred" Compromise. It could not be denied that this was the better course, if it were practicable; and accordingly, January 16, 1854, Senator Dixon of Kentucky offered an amendment to the pending Nebraska bill, which substantially embodied the repeal. In the Senate Douglas was chairman of the Committee on Territories, and was induced to coöperate. January 23, 1854, he introduced his famous "Kansas-Nebraska bill," establishing the two Territories and declaring the Missouri Compromise "inoperative" therein. A later amendment declared the Compromise to be "inconsistent with the principle of non-intervention by Congress with slavery in the States and Territories, as recognized by the legislation of 1850," and therefore "inoperative and void; it being the true intent and meaning of this Act not to legislate slavery into any Territory or State, nor to exclude it therefrom, but to leave the people thereof perfectly free to form and regulate their domestic institutions in their own way, subject only to the Constitution." After a long and hard fight the bill was passed with this clause in it, which Benton well stigmatized as a "stump speech injected into the belly of the bill." The insertion of the word State was of momentous significance.

This repeal set the anti-slavery party all ablaze. Among the rest Lincoln was fired with strenuous indignation, and roused from the condition of apparent indifference to public affairs in which he had rested since the close of his term in Congress. Douglas, coming home in the autumn, was so disagreeably received by an angry audience in Chicago that he felt it imperative to rehabilitate his stricken popularity. This difficult task he essayed at the great gathering of the State Fair in October. But Lincoln was put forward to answer him, and was brilliantly successful in doing so, if the highly colored account of Mr. Herndon may be trusted. Immediately after Lincoln's close, Owen Lovejoy, the Abolitionist leader, announced "a meeting in the same place that evening of all the friends of freedom." The scheme was to induce Lincoln to address them, and thus publicly to commit him as of their faith. But the astute Herndon, though himself an Abolitionist, felt that for Lincoln personally this was by no means desirable. So he hastened to Lincoln and strenuously said: "Go home at once! Take Bob with you, and drive somewhere into the country, and stay till this thing is over;" and Lincoln did take Bob and drove away to Tazewell Court House "on business." Herndon congratulates himself upon having "saved Lincoln," since either joining, or refusing to join, the Abolitionists at that time would have been attended with "great danger." Lincoln had upon his own part a wise instinct and a strong purpose to keep hard by Douglas and to close with him as often as opportunity offered. Soon afterward the two encountered again, and on this occasion it is narrated that Lincoln gave Douglas so much trouble that Douglas cried for a truce, proposing that neither of them should make any more speeches that autumn, to which Lincoln good-naturedly assented.

During this winter Lincoln was elected to the state legislature, but contrary to his own wish. For he designed to be a candidate for the United States Senate, and there might be a question as to his eligibility if he remained a member of the electing body. Accordingly he resigned his seat, which, to his surprise and chagrin, was immediately filled by a Democrat; for there was a reaction in Sangamon County. On February 8, 1855, the legislature began voting to elect a senator. The "Douglas Democrats" wished to reëlect Shields, the present incumbent. The first ballot stood, Lincoln, 45, Shields, 41, Lyman Trumbull, 5, scattering, 5 (or, according to other authority, 8). After several ballots Shields was thrown over in favor of a more "practicable" candidate, Governor Matteson, a "quasi-independent," who, upon the ninth ballot, showed a strength of 47, while Trumbull had 35, Lincoln had run down to 15, and "scattering" caught 1. Lincoln's weakness lay in the fact that the Abolitionists had too loudly praised him and publicly counted him as one of themselves. For this reason five Democrats, disgusted with Douglas for his attack on the Missouri Compromise, but equally bitter against Abolitionism, stubbornly refused ever to vote for a Whig, above all a Whig smirched by Abolitionist applause. So it seemed that Owen Lovejoy and his friends had incumbered Lincoln with a fatal handicap. The situation was this: Lincoln could count upon his fifteen adherents to the extremity; but the five anti-Douglas Democrats were equally stanch against him, so that his chance was evidently gone. Trumbull was a Democrat, but he was opposed to the policy of Douglas's Kansas-Nebraska bill; his following was not altogether trustworthy, and a trifling defection from it seemed likely to occur and to make out Matteson's majority. Lincoln pondered briefly; then, subjecting all else to the great principle of "anti-Nebraska," he urged his friends to transfer their votes to Trumbull. With grumbling and reluctance they did so, and by this aid, on the tenth ballot, Trumbull was elected. In a letter to Washburne, Lincoln wrote: "I think you would have done the same under the circumstances, though Judge Davis, who came down this morning, declares he never would have consented to the 47 men being controlled by the 5. I regret my defeat moderately, but am not nervous about it." If that was true which was afterwards so frequently reiterated by Douglas during the campaign of 1858, that a bargain had been struck between Lincoln and Trumbull, whereby the former was to succeed Shields and the latter was to succeed Douglas at the election two years later, then Lincoln certainly displayed on this occasion a "generosity" which deserves more than the very moderate praise which has been given it, of being "above the range of the mere politician's vision."

An immediate effect of this repealing legislation of 1854 was to cast Kansas into the arena as booty to be won in the fight between anti-slavery and pro-slavery. For this competition the North had the advantage that its population outnumbered that of the South in the ratio of three to two, and emigration was in accord with the habits of the people. Against this the South

It is an instance of Lincoln's political foresight that nearly two years and a half before this condition of affairs came about he had written: "If Kansas fairly votes herself a slave State, she must be admitted, or the Union must be dissolved."

offset proximity, of which the peculiar usefulness soon became apparent. Then was quickly under way a fair fight, in a certain sense, but most unfairly fought. Each side contended after its fashion; Northern anti-slavery merchants subscribed money to pay the expenses of free-state immigrants. "Border ruffians" and members of "Blue Lodges" and of kindred fraternities came across the border from Missouri to take a hand in every politico-belligerent crisis. The parties were not unequally matched; by temperament the free-state men were inclined to orderly and legitimate ways, yet they were willing and able to fight fire with fire. On the other hand, the slave-state men had a native preference for the bowie-knife and the shot-gun, yet showed a kind of respect for the ballot-box by insisting that it should be stuffed with votes on their side. Thus for a long while was waged a dubious, savage, and peculiar warfare. Imprisonments and rescues, beatings, shootings, plunderings, burnings, sieges, and lootings of towns were interspersed with elections of civil officers, with legislative enactments in ordinary form, with trials, suits at law, legal arguments, and decisions of judges. It is impossible here to sketch in detail this strange phantasmagory of arson, bloodshed, politics, and law.

Meantime other occurrences demand mention. In May, 1854, the seizure in Boston of Anthony Burns, as an escaped slave, caused a riot in which the court-house was attacked by a mob, one of the assailants was killed, and the militia were called out. Other like seizures elsewhere aroused the indignation of people who, whatever were their abstract theories as to the law, revolted at the actual spectacle of a man dragged back from freedom into slavery. May 22, 1856, Preston S. Brooks strode suddenly upon Charles Sumner, seated and unarmed at his desk in the senate-chamber, and beat him savagely over the head with a cane, inflicting very serious injuries. Had it been a fair fight, or had the South repudiated the act, the North might have made little of it, for Sumner was too advanced in his views to be politically popular. But, although the onslaught was even more offensive for its cowardice than for its brutality, nevertheless the South overwhelmed Brooks with laudation, and by so doing made thousands upon thousands of Republican votes at the North. The deed, the enthusiastic greeting, and the angry resentment marked the alarming height to which the excitement had risen.

The presidential campaign of the following summer, 1856, showed a striking disintegration and re-formation of political groups. Nominally there were four parties in the field: Democrats, Whigs, Native Americans or Know-Nothings, and Republicans. The Know-Nothings had lately won some state elections, but were of little account as a national organization, for they stood upon an issue hopelessly insignificant in comparison with slavery. Already many had gone over to the Republican camp; those who remained nominated as their candidates Millard Fillmore and Andrew J. Donelson. The Whigs were the feeble remnant of a really dead party, held together by affection for the old name; too few to do anything by themselves, they took by adoption the Know-Nothing candidates. The Republican party had been born only in 1854. Its members, differing on other matters, united upon the one doctrine, which they accepted as a test: opposition to the extension of slavery. They nominated John C. Fremont and William L. Dayton, and made a platform whereby they declared it to be "both the right and the duty of Congress to prohibit in the Territories those twin relics of barbarism, polygamy and slavery;" by which vehement and abusive language they excited the bitter resentment of the Southern Democracy. In this convention 110 votes were cast for Lincoln for the second place on the ticket. Lamon tells the little story that when this was told to Lincoln he replied that he could not have been the person designated, who was, doubtless, "the great Lincoln from Massachusetts." In the Democratic party there were two factions. The favorite candidate of the South was Franklin Pierce, for reëlection, with Stephen A. Douglas as a substitute or second choice; the North more generally preferred James Buchanan, who was understood to be displeased with the repeal of the Missouri Compromise. The struggle was sharp, but was won by the friends of Buchanan, with whom John C. Breckenridge was coupled. The campaign was eager, for the Republicans soon developed a strength beyond what had been expected and which put the Democrats to their best exertions. The result was

	Democrats.	Republicans.	Know-Nothings and Whigs.
Popular vote	1,838,169	1,341,264	874,534
Electoral vote	174	114	8

Thus James Buchanan became President of the United States, March 4, 1857,—stigmatized somewhat too severely as "a Northern man with Southern principles;" in fact an honest man and of good abilities, who, in ordinary times, would have left a fair reputation as a statesman of the second rank; but a man hopelessly unfit alike in character and in mind either to comprehend the present emergency or to rise to its demands. Yet, while the Democrats triumphed, the Republicans enjoyed the presage of the future; they had polled a total number of votes which surprised every one; on the other hand, the Democrats had lost ten States which they had carried in 1852 and had gained only two others, showing a net loss of eight States; and their electoral votes had dwindled from 254 to 174.

On the day following Buchanan's inauguration that occurred which had been foreshadowed with ill-advised plainness in his inaugural address. In the famous case of Dred Scott, the Supreme Court of the United States established as law the doctrine lately advanced by the Southern Democrats, that a slave was "property," and that his owner was entitled to be protected in the possession of him, as such, in the Territories. This necessarily demolished the rival theory of "popular sovereignty," which the Douglas Democrats had adopted, not without shrewdness, as being far better suited to the Northern mind. For clearly the people enjoyed no sovereignty where they had no option. Consequently in the Territories there was no longer a slavery question. The indignation of anti-slavery men of all shades of opinion was intense, and was unfortunately justifiable. For wholly apart from the controversy as to whether the law was better expounded by the chief justice or by Judge Curtis in his dissenting opinion, there remained a main fact, undeniable and inexcusable, to wit: that the court, having decided that the lower court had no jurisdiction, and being therefore itself unable to remand the cause for a new trial, had then outstepped its own proper function and outraged legal propriety by determining the questions raised by the rest of the record,—questions which no longer had any real standing before this tribunal. This course was well known to have been pursued with the purpose on the part of the majority of the judges to settle by judicial authority, and by a *dictum* conspicuously *obiter*, that great slavery question with which Congress had grappled in vain. It was a terrible blunder, for the people were only incensed by a volunteered and unauthorized interference. Moreover, the reasoning of Chief Justice Taney was such that the Republicans began anxiously to inquire why it was not as applicable to States as to Territories, and why it must not be extended to States when occasion should arrive; and in this connection it seemed now apparent why "States" had been named in the bill which repealed the Missouri Compromise. In spite of this menace the struggle in Kansas was not slackened. Time had been counting heavily in favor of the North. Her multitudinous population ceaselessly fed the stream of immigrants, and they were stubborn fellows who came to stay, and therefore were sure to wear out the persistence of the boot-and-saddle men from over the Missouri border. Accordingly, in 1857, the free-state men so

vastly outnumbered the slavery contingent, that even pro-slavery men had to
acknowledge it. Then the slavery party made its last desperate effort. Toward
the close of that year the Lecompton Constitution was framed by a convention
chosen at an election in which the free-state men, perhaps unwisely, had refused
to take part. When this pro-slavery instrument was offered to the people, they
were not allowed to vote simply Yea or Nay, but only "for the Constitution with
slavery," or "for the Constitution with no slavery." Again the free-state men
refrained from voting, and on December 21, 6,143 ballots were declared to have
been cast "for the Constitution with slavery," and 589 "for the Constitution with
no slavery." Much more than one third of the 6,143 were proved to be
fraudulent, but the residue far exceeded the requisite majority. January 4, 1858,
state officers were to be chosen, and now the free-state men decided to make an
irregular opportunity to vote, in their turn, simply for or against the Lecompton
Constitution. This time the pro-slavery men, considering the matter already
lawfully settled, refused to vote, and the result was that this polling showed
10,226 against the Constitution, 138 for the Constitution with slavery, 24 for
the Constitution without slavery. It is an instance of Lincoln's political foresight
that nearly two years and a half before this condition of affairs came about he
had written: "If Kansas fairly votes herself a slave State, she must be admitted,
or the Union must be dissolved. But how if she votes herself a slave State
unfairly?... Must she still be admitted, or the Union be dissolved? That will be
the phase of the question when it first becomes a practical one."

The struggle was now transferred to Washington. President Buchanan had
solemnly pledged himself to accept the result of the popular vote. Now he was
confronted by two popular votes, of which the one made somewhat the better
technical and formal showing, and the other undeniably expressed the true will
of a large majority of lawful voters. He selected the former, and advised
Congress to admit Kansas under the Lecompton Constitution with slavery. But
Douglas took the other side. The position of Douglas in the nation and in the
Democratic party deserves brief consideration, for in a way it was the cause of
Lincoln's nomination as the Republican candidate for the presidency in 1860.
From 1852 to 1860 Douglas was the most noteworthy man in public life in the
country. Webster, Clay, and Calhoun had passed away. Seward, Chase, and

Sumner, still in the earlier stages of their brilliant careers, were organizing the great party of the future. This interval of eight years belonged to Douglas more than to any other one man. He had been a candidate for the Democratic nomination for the presidency in 1852 and again in 1856; and had failed to secure it in part by reason of that unwritten rule whereby the leading statesmen are so often passed over, in order to confer the great prize upon insignificant and therefore presumably submissive men. Douglas was not of this type; he had high spirit, was ambitious, masterful, and self-confident; he was also an aggressive, brilliant, and tireless fighter in a political campaign, an orator combining something of the impressiveness of Webster with the readiness and roughness of the stump speaker. He had a thorough familiarity with all the

Douglas had as good a right as any man to the more dignified title of statesman.

politics, both the greater and the smaller, of the time; he was shrewd and adroit as a politician, and he had as good a right as any man then prominent in public life to the more dignified title of statesman. He had the art of popularity, and upon sufficient occasion could be supple and accommodating even in the gravest matters of principle. He had always been a Democrat. He now regarded himself as properly the leader of the Democratic party; and of course he still aimed at the high office which he had twice missed. With this object in view, he had gone very far to retain his hold upon the South. He told Southerners that by his happy theory of "popular sovereignty" he had educated the public mind, and accomplished the repeal of the Missouri Compromise. When the Dred Scott decision took the life out of his "popular sovereignty," he showed his wonted readiness in adapting himself to the situation. To the triumphant South he graciously admitted the finality of a decision which sustained the most extreme Southern doctrine. To the perturbed and indignant North he said cheeringly that the decision was of no practical consequence whatsoever! For every one knew that slavery could not exist in any community without the aid of friendly legislation; and if any anti-slavery community should by its anti-slavery legisluture withhold this essential friendly legislation, then slavery in that State might be lawful but would be impossible. So, he said, there is still in fact "popular sovereignty."

When the pro-slavery Lecompton Constitution came up for consideration Douglas decided not to rest content with the form of popular approval, but to stand out for the substance. He quarreled with Buchanan, and in an angry interview they exchanged threats and defiance. Douglas felt himself the greater man of the two in the party, and audaciously indicated something like contempt for the rival who was not leader but only President. Conscience, if one may be allowed gravely to speak of the conscience of a professional politician, and policy were in comfortable unison in commending this choice to Douglas. For his term as senator was to expire in 1858, and reëlection was not only in itself desirable, but seemed essential to securing the presidency in 1860. Heretofore Illinois had been a Democratic State; the southern part, peopled by immigrants from neighboring slave States, was largely pro-slavery; but the northern part, containing the rapidly growing city of Chicago, had been filled from the East, and was inclined to sympathize with the rest of the North. Such being the situation, an avowal of Democratic principles, coupled with the repudiation of the Lecompton fraud, seemed the shrewd and safe course in view of Douglas's political surroundings, also the consistent, or may we say honest, course in view of his antecedent position. If, in thus retaining his hold on Illinois, he gave to the Southern Democracy an offense which could never be forgotten or forgiven, this misfortune was due to the impracticable situation and not to any lack of skillful strategy on his part. In spite of him the bill passed the Senate, but in the House twenty-two Northern Democrats went over to the opposition, and carried a substitute measure, which established that the Lecompton Constitution must again be submitted to popular vote. Though this was done by the body of which Douglas was not a member, yet every one felt that it was in fact his triumph over the administration. A Committee of Conference then brought in the "English bill." Under this the Kansans were to vote, August 3, 1858, either to accept the pro-slavery Lecompton Constitution, with the *douceur* of a land grant, or to reject it. If they accepted it, the State was to be admitted at once; if they rejected it, they were not to be admitted until the population should reach the number which was required for electing a member to the House of Representatives. At present the population was far short of this number, and therefore rejection involved a long delay in acquiring statehood. Douglas very justly assailed the unfairness of a proposal by which an anti-slavery vote was thus doubly and very severely handicapped; but the bill was passed by both Houses of Congress and was signed by the President. The Kansans, however, by an enormous majority, rejected the bribes of land and statehood in connection with slavery. For his action concerning the Lecompton Constitution and the "English bill" Douglas afterward took much credit to himself.

Such was the stage of advancement of the slavery conflict in the country, and such the position of Douglas in national and in state politics, when there took place that great campaign in Illinois which made him again senator in 1858, and made Lincoln President in 1860.

CHAPTER V

THE LINCOLN-DOUGLAS JOINT DEBATE

Illinois State Capitol

*"Either the opponents of slavery will
arrest the further spread of it…or its
advocates will push it forward, till it shall
become alike lawful in all the States."*

About this time Lincoln again became active in the politics of his State, aiding in the formation of the Republican party there. On May 29, 1856, a state convention of "all opponents of anti-Nebraska legislation" was held at Bloomington. After "a platform ringing with strong anti-Nebraska sentiments" had been adopted, Lincoln, "in response to repeated calls, came forward and delivered a speech of such earnestness and power that no one who heard it will ever forget the effect it produced." It was "never written out or printed," which is to be regretted; but it lives in one of those vivid descriptions by Herndon which leave nothing to the imagination. For the moment this triumph was gratifying; but when Lincoln, leaving the hot enthusiasts of Bloomington, came home to his fellow townsmen at Springfield, he passed into a chill atmosphere of indifference and disapproval. An effort was made to gather a mass meeting in order to ratify the action of the state convention. But

It was one of those periods in which small men are laid aside and great leaders are recognized by popular instinct; when the little band that is in deepest earnest becomes endowed with a force which compels the mass of careless, temporizing human-kind to gravitate towards it.

the "mass" consisted of three persons, viz., Abraham Lincoln, Herndon, and one John Pain. It was trying, but Lincoln was finely equal to the occasion; in a few words, passing from jest to earnest, he said that the meeting was larger than he *knew* it would be; for while he knew that he and his partner would attend, he was not sure of any one else; and yet another man had been found brave enough to come out. But, "while all seems dead, the age itself is not. It liveth as sure as our Maker liveth. Under all this seeming want of life and motion the world does move, nevertheless. Be hopeful, and now let us adjourn and appeal to the people!"

In the presidential campaign of 1856 the Republicans of Illinois put Lincoln on their electoral ticket, and he entered into the campaign promptly and very zealously. Traveling untiringly to and fro, he made about fifty speeches. By the quality of these, even more than by their number, he became the champion of the party, so that pressing demands for him came from the neighboring States. He was even heard of in the East. But there he encountered a lack of appreciation and in some quarters an hostility which he felt to be hurtful to his prospects as well as unjust towards a leading Republican of the Northwest. Horace Greeley, enthusiastic, well meaning, ever blundering, the editor of the New York "Tribune," cast the powerful influence of that sheet against him; and as the senatorial contest of 1858 was approaching, in which Lincoln hoped to be a principal, this ill feeling was very unfortunate. "I fear," he said, "that Greeley's attitude will damage me with Sumner, Seward, Wilson, Phillips, and other friends in the East,"—and by the way, it is interesting to note this significant list of political "friends." Thereupon Herndon, as guardian of Lincoln's political prospects, went to pass the opening months of the important year upon a crusade among the great men of the East, designing to extinguish the false lights erroneously hung out by persons ignorant of the truth. Erelong he cheered Lincoln by encouraging accounts of success, and of kind words spoken by many Eastern magnates.

In 1858, ability, courage, activity, ambition, the prestige of success, and a plausible moderation in party politics combined to make Douglas the most conspicuous individual in the public view. There was no other way whereby any other man could so surely attract the close and interested attention of the whole people as by meeting Douglas in direct personal competition. If Douglas had not held the position which he did, or if, holding it, he had lived in another State than Illinois, Lincoln might never have been President of the United States. But the essential facts lay favorably for effecting that presentation before the people which was indispensable for his fortunes. In April, 1858, the Democratic State Convention of Illinois indorsed the position which Douglas had taken in the Kansas business. This involved that the party should present him as its candidate for reëlection to the national Senate by the legislature whose members were to be chosen in the following autumn. "In the very nature of things," says the enthusiastic Herndon, Lincoln was at once selected by the Republicans, and on June 16 their convention resolved that "Hon. Abraham Lincoln is our first and only choice for United States senator to fill the vacancy about to be created by the expiration of Mr. Douglas's term of office." Immediately the popular excitement gave measure of the estimate placed upon the two men by those who most accurately knew their qualities. All Illinoisians looked forward eagerly to the fine spectacle of a battle royal between real leaders.

The general political condition was extremely confused. The great number of worthy citizens, who had been wont to save themselves from the worry of critical thought in political matters by the simple process of uniform allegiance to a party, now found the old familiar organizations rapidly disintegrating. They were dismayed and bewildered at the scene; everywhere there were new cries, new standards, new leaders, while small bodies of recruits, displaying in strange union old comrades beside old foes, were crossing to and fro and changing relationships, to the inextricable confusion of the situation. In such a chaos each man was driven to do his own thinking, to discover his genuine beliefs, and to determine in what company he could stand enduringly in the troublous times ahead. It was one of those periods in which small men are laid aside and great leaders are recognized by popular instinct; when the little band that is in deepest earnest becomes endowed with a force which compels the mass of careless, temporizing human-kind to gravitate towards it. Such bands were now the Abolitionists at the North and the Secessionists at the South. Between them lay the nation, disquieted, contentious, and more than a little angry at the prevalent discomfort and alarm. At the North nine men out of ten cared far less for any principle, moral or political, than they did for the discovery of some course whereby this unwelcome conflict between slavery and freedom could be prevented from disorganizing the course of daily life and business; and since the Abolitionists were generally charged with being in great measure responsible for the present menacing condition, they were regarded with bitter animosity by a large number of their fellow citizens. The Secessionists were not in equal disfavor at the South, yet they were still very much in the minority, even in the Gulf States.

Illinois had been pretty stanchly Democratic in times past, but no one could forecast the complexion which she would put on in the coming campaign.

The Whigs were gone. The Republican party, though so lately born, yet had already traversed the period of infancy and perhaps also that of youth; men guessed wildly how many voters would now cast its ballot. On the other hand, the Democrats were suffering from internal quarrels. The friends of Douglas, and all moderate Democrats, declared him to be the leader of the Democracy; but Southern conventions and newspapers were angrily "reading him out" of the

Frequently he stopped short to jot down an idea or expression upon some scrap of paper, which then he thrust into his hat. Thus, piece by piece, the accumulation grew alike inside and outside of his head, and at last he took all his fragments and with infinite consideration moulded them into unity.

party, and the singular spectacle was witnessed of the Democratic administration sending out its orders to all Federal office-holders in Illinois to oppose the Democratic nominee, even to the point of giving the election to the Republicans; for if discipline was to exist, a defection like that of which Douglas had been guilty must be punished with utter and everlasting destruction at any cost. This schism of course made the numerical uncertainties even more uncertain than they rightfully should have been. Yet, in an odd way, the same fact worked also against Lincoln; for Douglas's recent votes against the pro-slavery measures of the administration for the admission of Kansas, together with his own direct statements on recent occasions, had put him in a light which misled many Northern anti-slavery men, whose perception did not penetrate to the core-truth. For example, not only Greeley, but Henry Wilson, Burlingame, Washburne, Colfax, and more, really believed that Douglas was turning his back upon his whole past career, and that this brilliant political strategist was actually bringing into the anti-slavery camp all his accumulations of prestige, popularity, and experience, all his seductive eloquence, his skill, and his grand mastery over men. Blinded by the dazzling prospect, they gave all their influence in favor of this priceless recruit, forgetting that, if he were in fact such an apostate as they believed him to be, he would come to them terribly shrunken in value and trustworthiness. Some even were so infatuated as to insist that the Republicans of Illinois ought to present no candidate against him. Fortunately the Illinoisians knew their fellow citizen better; yet in so strange a jumble no one could deny that it was a doubtful conflict in which these two rivals were joining.

Lincoln had expected to be nominated, and during several weeks he had been thinking over his speech of acceptance. However otherwise he might seem at any time to be engaged, he was ceaselessly turning over this matter in his mind; and frequently he stopped short to jot down an idea or expression upon some scrap of paper, which then he thrust into his hat. Thus, piece by piece, the accumulation grew alike inside and outside of his head, and at last he took all his fragments and with infinite consideration moulded them into unity. So studiously had he wrought that by the time of delivery he had unconsciously committed the whole speech accurately to memory. If so much painstaking seemed to indicate an exaggerated notion of the importance of his words, he was soon vindicated by events; for what he said was subjected to a dissection and a criticism such as have not often pursued the winged words of the orator. When at last the composition was completed, he gathered a small coterie of his friends and admirers, and read it to them. The opening paragraph was as follows:—

> "If we could first know where we are, and whither we are tending, we could better judge what to do and how to do it. We are now far into the fifth year since a policy was initiated with the avowed object and confident promise of putting an end to slavery agitation. Under the operation of that policy, that agitation has not only not ceased, but has constantly augmented. In my opinion, it will not cease until a crisis shall have been reached and passed. 'A house divided against itself cannot stand.' I believe this government cannot endure permanently half slave and half free. I do not expect the

Union to be dissolved,—I do not expect the house to fall,—
but I do expect it will cease to be divided. It will become all
one thing or all the other. Either the opponents of slavery will
arrest the further spread of it, and place it where the public
mind shall rest in the belief that it is in the course of ultimate
extinction; or its advocates will push it forward, till it shall
become alike lawful in all the States, old as well as new,—
North as well as South."

As the reader watched for the effect of this exordium he only saw disapproval
and consternation. His assembled advisers and critics, each and all save only the
fiery Herndon, protested that language so daring and advanced would work a ruin
that might not be mended in years. Lincoln heard their condemnation with
gravity rather than surprise. But he had worked his way to a conviction, and he
was immovable; all he said was, that the statement was true, right, and just, that it
was time it should be made, and that he would make it, even though he might
have "to go down with it;" that he would "rather be defeated with this expression
in the speech ... than to be victorious without it." Accordingly, on the next day he
spoke the paragraph without the change of a word.

It is not without effort that we can now appreciate fully why this utterance
was so momentous in the spring of 1858. By it Lincoln came before the people
with a plain statement of precisely that which more than nine hundred and
ninety-nine persons in every thousand, especially at the North, were striving
with all their might to stamp down as an untruth; he said to them what they all
were denying with desperation, and with rage against the asserters. Their
bitterness was the greater because very many, in the bottom of their hearts,
distrusted their own painful and strenuous denial. No words could be more
unpopular than that the divided house could not permanently stand, when the
whole nation was insisting, with the intensity of despair, that it could stand,
would stand, must stand. Consequently occurrences soon showed his friends to
be right so far as concerned the near, practical point: that the paragraph would
cost more voters in Illinois than Lincoln could lose without losing his election.
But beyond that point, a little farther away in time, much deeper down amid

enduring results, Lincoln's judgment was ultimately seen to rest upon fundamental wisdom, politically as well as morally. For Lincoln was no idealist, sacrificing realities to abstractions; on the contrary, the right which he saw was always a practical right, a right which could be compassed. In this instance, the story goes that he retorted upon some of those who grumbled about his "mistake," that in time they "would consider it the wisest thing he ever said." In this he foretold truly; that daring and strong utterance was the first link in the chain of which a more distant link lay across the threshold of the White House.

A battle opened by so resounding a shot was sure to be furious. Writers and speakers fell upon the fateful paragraph and tore it savagely. They found in it a stimulus which, in fact, was not needed; for already were present all the

When he had found a form which satisfied him for the expression of a conviction, he was apt to use it repeatedly rather than to seek new and varied shapes, so that substantially identical sentences often recur at distant intervals of time and place.

elements of the fiercest struggle,—the best man and the best fighter in each party at the front, and not unevenly matched; a canvass most close and doubtful; and a question which stirred the souls of men with the passions of crusading days. Douglas added experience and distinction to gallantry in attack, adroitness in defense, readiness in personalities, and natural aptitude for popular oratory. Lincoln frankly admitted his formidable qualifications. But the Republican managers had a shrewd appreciation of both opponents; they saw that Lincoln's forte lay in hitting out straight, direct, and hard; and they felt that blows of the kind he delivered should not go out into the air, but should alight upon a concrete object,—upon Douglas. They conceived a wise plan. On July 24, 1858, Lincoln challenged Douglas to a series of joint debates. Douglas accepted, and named seven meetings, which he so arranged that he opened and closed four times and Lincoln opened and closed three times; but Lincoln made no point of the inequality; the arrangement was completed, and this famous duel constituted another link in that White House chain.

The setting of the spectacle had the picturesqueness of the times and the region. The people gathered in vast multitudes, to the number of ten thousand, even of twenty thousand, at the places named for the speech-making; they came in their wagons from all the country round, bringing provisions, and making camps in the groves and fields. There were bonfires and music, parading and drinking. He was a singular man in Illinois who was not present at some one of these encounters.

Into a competition so momentous Lincoln entered with a full appreciation of the burden and responsibility which it put upon him. He had at once to meet a false gloss of his famous sentence; and though he had been very precise and accurate in his phraseology for the express purpose of escaping misinterpretation, yet it would have been a marvel in applied political morals if the paraphrases devised by Douglas had been strictly ingenuous. The favorite distortion was to alter what was strictly a forecast into a declaration of a policy, to make a prediction pass for an avowal of a purpose to wage war against slavery until either the "institution" or "Abolitionism" should be utterly defeated and forever exterminated. It was said to be a "doctrine" which was "revolutionary and destructive of this government," and which "invited a warfare between the North and the South, to be carried on with ruthless vengeance, until the one section or the other shall be driven to the wall and become the victim of the rapacity of the other." Such misrepresentation annoyed Lincoln all the more because it was undeserved. The history of the utterance thus maltreated illustrates the deliberate, cautious, thorough way in which his mind worked. So long ago as August 15, 1855, he had closed a letter with the paragraph: "Our political problem now is: Can we, as a nation, continue together *permanently— forever,* half slave and half free? The problem is too mighty for me. May God in his mercy superintend the solution." This is one among many instances which show how studiously Lincoln pondered until he had got his conclusion into that simple shape in which it was immutable. When he had found a form which satisfied him for the expression of a conviction, he was apt to use it repeatedly rather than to seek new and varied shapes, so that substantially identical sentences often recur at distant intervals of time and place.

When one has been long studying with much earnest intensity of thought a perplexing and moving question, and at last frames a conclusion with painstaking precision in perfectly clear language, it is not pleasant to have that accurate utterance misstated with tireless reiteration, and with infinite art and plausibility. But for this vexation Lincoln could find no remedy, and it was in vain that he again and again called attention to the fact that he had expressed neither a "doctrine," nor an "invitation," nor any "purpose" or policy whatsoever. But as it seemed not altogether courageous to leave his position in doubt, he said: "Now, it is singular enough, if you will carefully read that passage over, that I did not say in it that I was in favor of anything. I only said what I expected would take place.... I did not even say that I desired that slavery should be put in course of ultimate extinction. I do say so now, however, so there need be no longer any difficulty about that." He felt that nothing short of such extinction would surely prevent the revival of a dispute which had so often been settled "*forever*." "We can no more foretell," he said, "where the end of this slavery agitation will be than we can see the end of the world itself.... There is no way of putting an end to the slavery agitation amongst us but to put it back upon the basis where our fathers placed it.... Then the public mind will rest in the belief that it is in the course of ultimate extinction."

There was much of this eloquence about "the fathers," much evocation of the shades of the great departed, who, having reached the eternal silence, could be claimed by both sides. The contention was none the less strenuous because it was entirely irrelevant; since the opinion of "the fathers" could not make slavery right or wrong. Many times therefore did Douglas charge Lincoln with having said "that the Union could not endure divided as our fathers made it, with free and slave States;" as though this were a sort of blasphemy against the national demigods. Lincoln aptly retorted that, as matter of fact, these same distinguished "fathers"—"Washington, Jefferson, Franklin, Madison, Hamilton, Jay, and the great men of that day"—did not *make*, but *found*, the nation half slave and half free; that they set "many clear marks of disapprobation" upon slavery, and left it so situated that the popular mind rested in the belief that it was in the course of ultimate extinction. Unfortunately it had not been allowed to remain as they had left it; but on the contrary, "all the trouble and convulsion has proceeded from the efforts to spread it over more territory."

Pursuing this line, Lincoln alleged the purpose of the pro-slavery men to make slavery "perpetual and universal" and "national." In his great speech of acceptance at Springfield he put this point so well that he never improved upon this first presentation of it. The repeal of the Missouri Compromise in 1854 "opened all the national territory to slavery, and was the first point gained. But so far Congress only had acted, and an indorsement by the people, real or imaginary," was obtained by "the notable argument of 'squatter sovereignty,'

The Supreme Court had interpreted the Constitution, and Lincoln was inciting the people to annul that interpretation by some political process not known to the law.

otherwise called 'sacred right of self-government,' which latter phrase, though expressive of the only rightful basis of any government, was so perverted in this attempted use of it as to amount to just this: that if any one man choose to enslave *another*, no *third* man shall be permitted to object. That argument was incorporated into the Nebraska bill." In May, 1854, this bill was passed. Then the presidential election came. "Mr. Buchanan was elected, and the indorsement was secured. That was the second point gained." Meantime the celebrated case of the negro, Dred Scott, was pending in the Supreme Court, and the "President in his inaugural address fervently exhorted the people to abide by the forthcoming decision, whatever it might be. Then in a few days came the decision," which was at once emphatically indorsed by Douglas, "the reputed author of the Nebraska bill," and by the new President.

"At length a squabble springs up between the President and the author of the Nebraska bill on the mere question of *fact*, whether the Lecompton Constitution was or was not, in any just sense, made by the people of Kansas; and in that quarrel the latter declares that all he wants is a fair vote for the people, and that he cares not whether slavery be voted *down* or voted *up*.

.   .   .   .

"The several points of the Dred Scott decision in connection with Senator Douglas's 'care not' policy constitute the piece of machinery in its present state of advancement. This was the third point gained.

.   .   .   .

"We cannot absolutely know that all these exact adaptations are the result of preconcert. But when we see a lot of framed timbers, different portions of which we know have been gotten out at different times and places and by different workmen, —Stephen, Franklin, Roger, and James, for instance,—and when we see these timbers joined together, and see they exactly make the frame of a house or a mill, all the tenons and mortices exactly fitting, and all the

Lincoln countered by asking: Was it, then, the case that it was slavery which was national, and freedom which was sectional?

lengths and proportions of the different pieces exactly adapted to their respective places, and not a piece too many or too few,—not omitting even scaffolding; or, if a single piece be lacking, we see the place in the frame exactly fitted and prepared yet to bring such piece in,—in such a case, we find it impossible not to believe that Stephen and Franklin and Roger and James all understood one another from the beginning, and all worked upon a common plan or draft drawn up before the first blow was struck.

"It should not be overlooked that by the Nebraska bill the people of a *State* as well as a Territory were to be left 'perfectly free,' 'subject only to the

Constitution.' Why mention a *State*?... Why is mention of this lugged into this merely territorial law?

.   .   .   .

"Put this and that together, and we have another nice little niche, which we may erelong see filled with another Supreme Court decision, declaring that the Constitution of the United States does not permit a *State* to exclude slavery from its limits. And this may especially be expected if the doctrine of 'care not whether slavery be voted down or voted up' shall gain upon the public mind sufficiently to give promise that such a decision can be maintained when made. Such a decision is all that slavery now lacks of being alike lawful in all the States." Following out this idea, Lincoln repeatedly put to Douglas a question to which he could never get a direct answer from his nimble antagonist: "If a decision is made, holding that the people of the *States* cannot exclude slavery, will he support it, or not?"

Even so skillful a dialectician as Douglas found this compact structure of history and argument a serious matter. Its simple solidity was not so susceptible to treatment by the perverting process as had been the figurative and prophetic utterance about the "house divided against itself." Neither could he find a chink between the facts and the inferences. One aspect of the speech, however, could not be passed over. Lincoln said that he had not charged "Stephen and Franklin and Roger and James" with collusion and conspiracy; but he admitted that he had "arrayed the evidence tending to prove," and which he "thought did prove," these things. It was impossible for the four distinguished gentlemen who owned the rest of these names to refuse to plead. Accordingly Douglas sneered vehemently at the idea that two presidents, the chief justice, and he himself had been concerned in that grave crime against the State which was imputed to them; and when, by his lofty indignation, he had brought his auditors into sympathy, he made the only possible reply: that the real meaning, the ultimate logical outcome, of what Lincoln had said was, that a decision of the Supreme Court was to be set aside by the political action of the people at the polls. The Supreme Court had interpreted the Constitution, and Lincoln was inciting the people to annul that interpretation by some political process not known to the law. For himself, he proclaimed with effective emphasis his allegiance to that great tribunal in the performance of its constitutional duties. Lincoln replied that he also bowed to the Dred Scott decision in the specific case; but he repudiated it as a binding rule in political action. His point seemed more obscure than was usual with him, and not satisfactory as an answer to Douglas. But as matter of fact no one was deceived by the amusing adage of the profession: that the courts do not *make* the law, but only *declare what it is*. Every one knew that the law was just what the judges chose from time to time to say that it was, and that if judicial *declarations* of the law were not reversed quite so often as legislative makings of the law were repealed, it was only because the identity of a bench is usually of longer duration than the identity of a legislative body. If the people, politically, willed the reversal of the Dred Scott decision, it was sure in time to be judicially reversed.

Douglas boasted that the Democrats were a national party, whereas the "Black Republicans" were a sectional body whose creed could not be uttered south of Mason and Dixon's line. He was assiduous in fastening upon Lincoln the name of "Abolitionist," and "Black Republican," epithets so unpopular that those who held the faith often denied the title, and he only modified them by the offensive admission that Lincoln's doctrines were sometimes disingenuously weakened to suit certain audiences: "His principles in the north [of Illinois] are jet black; in the centre they are in color a decent mulatto; and in lower Egypt they are almost white."

Concerning sectionalism, Lincoln countered fairly enough on his opponent by asking: Was it, then, the case that it was slavery which was national, and freedom which was sectional? Or, "Is it the true test of the soundness of a doctrine that in some places people won't let you proclaim it?" But the remainder of Douglas's assault was by no means to be disposed of by quick retort. When Lincoln was pushed to formulate accurately his views concerning the proper status of the negro in the community, he had need of all his extraordinary care in statement. Herein lay problems that were vexing many honest citizens and clever men besides himself, and were breeding much disagreement among persons who all were anti-slavery in a general way, but could by no means reach a comfortable unison concerning troublesome particulars. The "all men free and equal" of the Constitution, and the talk about human brotherhood, gave the Democrats wide scope for harassing anti-slavery men with vexatious taunts and embarrassing cross-interrogatories on practical points. "I do not question," said Douglas, "Mr. Lincoln's conscientious belief that the negro was made his equal, and hence is his brother. But for my own part, I do not regard the negro as my equal, and positively deny that he is my brother, or any kin to me whatever." He said that "the signers of the Declaration had no reference to the negro,... or any other inferior and degraded race, when they spoke of the equality of men," but meant only "white men, of European

He thought slowly, cautiously, profoundly, and with a most close accuracy; but above all else he thought fairly.

birth and descent." This topic opens the whole subject of Lincoln's political affiliations and of his opinions concerning slavery and the negro, opinions which seem to have undergone no substantial change during the interval betwixt this campaign and his election to the presidency. Some selections from what he said may sufficiently explain his position.

At Freeport, August 27, replying to a series of questions from Douglas, he declared that he had supposed himself, "since the organization of the Republican party at Bloomington, in May, 1856, bound as a party man by the platforms of the party, then and since." He said: "I do not now, nor ever did, stand in favor of the unconditional repeal of the Fugitive Slave Law." He believed that under the Constitution the Southerners were entitled to such a law; but thought that the existing law "should have been framed so as to be free from some of the objections that pertain to it, without lessening its efficiency." He would not "introduce it as a new subject of agitation upon the general question of slavery."

He should be "exceedingly sorry" ever to have to pass upon the question of admitting more slave States into the Union, and exceedingly glad to know that another never would be admitted. But "if slavery shall be kept out of the Territories during the territorial existence of any one given Territory, and then the people shall, having a fair chance and a clear field, when they come to adopt their constitution, do such an extraordinary thing as to adopt a slave constitution, uninfluenced by the actual presence of the institution among them, I see no alternative, if we own the country, but to admit them into the Union." He should also, he said, be "exceedingly glad to see slavery abolished in the District of Columbia," and he believed that Congress had "constitutional power to abolish it" there; but he would favor the measure only upon condition: "First, that the abolition should be gradual; second, that it should be on a vote of the majority of qualified voters in the District; and, third, that compensation should be made to unwilling owners." As to the abolition of the slave trade between the different States, he acknowledged that he had not considered the matter sufficiently to have reached a conclusion concerning it. But if he should think that Congress had power to effect such abolition, he should "not be in favor of the exercise of that power unless upon some conservative principle, akin to what I have said in relation to the abolition of slavery in the District of Columbia." As to the territorial controversy, he said: "I am impliedly, if not expressly, pledged to a belief in the *right* and *duty* of Congress to prohibit slavery in all the United States Territories." Concerning the acquisition of new territory he said: "I am not generally opposed to honest acquisition of territory; and in any given case I would or would not oppose such acquisition, according as I might think such acquisition would or would not aggravate the slavery question among ourselves." The statement derived its immediate importance from the well-known purpose of the administration and a considerable party in the South very soon to acquire Cuba. All these utterances were certainly clear enough, and were far from constituting Abolitionist doctrine, though they were addressed to an audience "as strongly tending to Abolitionism as any audience in the State of Illinois," and Mr. Lincoln believed that he was saying "that which, if it would be offensive to any person and render them enemies to himself, would be offensive to persons in this audience."

At Quincy Lincoln gave his views concerning Republicanism with his usual unmistakable accuracy, and certainly he again differentiated it widely from Abolitionism. The Republican party, he said, think slavery "a moral, a social, and a political wrong." Any man who does not hold this opinion "is misplaced and ought to leave us. While, on the other hand, if there be any man in the Republican party who is impatient over the necessity springing from its actual presence, and is impatient of the constitutional guarantees thrown around it, and would act in disregard of these, he, too, is misplaced, standing with us. He will find his place somewhere else; for we have a due regard ... for all these things." ... "I have always hated slavery as much as any Abolitionist,... but I have always been quiet about it until this new era of the introduction of the Nebraska bill again." He repeated often that he had "no purpose, directly or indirectly, to interfere with the institution of slavery in the States where it exists;" that he had "no lawful right to do so," and "no inclination to do so." He said that his declarations as to the right of the negro to "life, liberty, and the pursuit of happiness" were designed only to refer to legislation "about any new country which is not already cursed with the actual presence of the evil,— slavery." He denied having ever "manifested any impatience with the necessities that spring from the ... actual existence of slavery among us, where it does already exist."

He dwelt much upon the equality clause of the Declaration. If we begin "making exceptions to it, where will it stop? If one man says it does not mean a negro, why not another say it does not mean some other man?" Only within three years past had any one doubted that negroes were included by this language. But he said that, while the authors "intended to include *all* men, they did not mean to declare all men equal *in all respects*,... in color, size, intellect, moral development, or social capacity," but only "equal in certain inalienable rights." "Anything that argues me into his [Douglas's] idea of perfect social and political equality with the negro is but a specious and fantastic arrangement of words, by which a man can prove a horse chestnut to be a chestnut horse.... I have no purpose to produce political and social equality between the white and the black races. There is a physical difference between the two, which, in my judgment, will probably forever forbid their living together upon the footing of perfect equality; and inasmuch as it becomes a necessity that there must be a difference, I, as well as Judge Douglas, am in favor of the race to which I belong having the superior position.... But I hold that ... there is no reason in the world why the negro is not entitled to all the natural rights enumerated in the Declaration of Independence, the right to life, liberty, and the pursuit of happiness. I hold that he is as much entitled to these as the white man. I agree with Judge Douglas that he is not my equal in many respects,—certainly not in color, perhaps not in moral or intellectual endowment. But in the right to eat the bread, without the leave of anybody else, which his own hand earns, *he is my equal, and the equal of Judge Douglas, and the equal of every living man.*" Later at

His effort never was to defeat the person who happened to be his adversary, but always was to overcome the arguments of that adversary.

Charleston he reiterated much of this in almost identical language, and then in his turn took his fling at Douglas: "I am not in favor of making voters or jurors of negroes, nor of qualifying them to hold office, nor to intermarry with white people.... I do not understand that because I do not want a negro woman for a slave I must necessarily want her for a wife. My understanding is that I can just let her alone.... I have never had the least apprehension that I or my friends would marry negroes, if there was no law to keep them from it; but as Judge Douglas and his friends seem to be in great apprehension that *they* might, if there were no law to keep them from it, I give him the most solemn pledge that I will to the very last stand by the law of this State, which forbids the marrying of white people with negroes."

By all this it is made entirely evident that Lincoln held a faith widely different from that of the great crusading leaders of Abolitionism at the East. Equally marked was the difference between him and them in the matters of temper and of the attitude taken towards opponents. The absence of any sense of personal hostility towards those who assailed him with unsparing vindictiveness was a trait often illustrated in his after life, and which was now noted with surprise, for it was rare in the excited politics of those days. In this especial campaign both contestants honestly intended to refrain from personalities, but the difference between their ways of doing so was marked. Douglas, under the temptation of high ability in that line, held himself in check by an effort which was often obvious and not always entirely successful. But Lincoln never seemed moved by the desire. "All I have to ask," he said, "is that we talk reasonably and rationally;" and again: "I hope to deal in all things fairly with Judge Douglas." No innuendo, no artifice, in any speech, gave the lie to these protestations. Besides this, his denunciations were always against *slavery*, and never against *slaveholders*. The emphasis of condemnation, the intensity of feeling, were never expended against persons. By this course, unusual among the Abolitionists, he not only lost nothing in force and impressiveness, but, on the contrary, his attack seemed to gain in effectiveness by being directed against no personal object, but exclusively against a practice. His war was against slavery, not against the men and women of the South who owned slaves. At Ottawa he read from the Peoria speech of 1854: "I have no prejudice against the Southern people. They are just what we would [should] be in their situation. If slavery did not now exist among them, they would not introduce it. If it did now exist among us, we should not instantly give it up.... It does seem to me that systems of gradual emancipation might be adopted; but for their tardiness in this, I will not undertake to judge our brethren of the South." Repeatedly he admitted the difficulty of the problem, and fastened no blame upon those Southerners who excused themselves for not expelling the evil on the ground that they did not know how to do so. At Peoria he said: "If all earthly power were given me, I should not know what to do as to the existing institution." He contributed some suggestions which certainly were nothing better than chimerical. Deportation to Africa was his favorite scheme; he also proposed that it would be "best for all concerned to have the colored population in a State by themselves." But he did not abuse men who declined to adopt his methods. Though he was dealing with a question which was arousing personal antagonisms as bitter as any that history records, yet he never condemned any one, nor ever passed judgment against his fellow men.

Diagnosis would perhaps show that the trait thus illustrated was mental rather than moral. This absence of animosity and reproach as towards individuals found its root not so much in human charity as in fairness of thinking. Lincoln's ways of mental working are not difficult to discover. He thought slowly, cautiously, profoundly, and with a most close accuracy; but above all else *he thought fairly*. This capacity far transcended, or, more correctly, differed from, what is ordinarily called the judicial habit of mind. Many men can weigh arguments without letting prejudice get into either scale; but Lincoln carried on the whole process of thinking, not only with an equal clearness of perception, but also with an entire impartiality of liking or disliking for both sides. His aim, while he was engaged in thinking, was to discover what was really true; and later when he spoke to others his purpose was to show them the truth which he had discovered, and to state to them on what grounds he believed it to be the truth; it did not involve a judgment against the individuals who failed to recognize that truth. His singular trait of impersonality was not made more apparent in any other way. His effort never was to defeat the person who happened to be his adversary, but always was to overcome the arguments of that adversary. Primarily he was discussing a topic and establishing a truth; it was only incidental that in doing these things he had to oppose a man. It is noteworthy that his opponents never charged him with misstating their case in order to make an apparently effective answer to it. On the contrary, his hope of success seemed always to lie in having both sides presented with the highest degree of clearness and honesty. He had perfect confidence in the ultimate triumph of the truth; he was always willing to tie fast to it, according as he could see it, and then to bide time with it. This being a genuine faith and not mere lip-service, he used the same arguments to others which he used to himself, and staked his final success upon the probability that what had persuaded his mind would in time persuade also the minds of other intelligent men. It has been well said of him by an excellent judge: "He loved the truth for the truth's sake. He would not argue from a false premise, or be deceived himself, or deceive others, by a false conclusion.... He did not seek to say merely the thing which was best for that day's debate, but the thing which would stand the test of time, and square itself with eternal justice.... His logic was severe and faultless. He did not resort to fallacy."

To return to the points made in the debate: Douglas laid down the "great principle of non-interference and non-intervention by Congress with slavery in the States and Territories alike;" which he assured his audience would enable us to "continue at peace with one another." In the same connection he endeavored to silver-coat for Northern palates the bitter pill of the Dred Scott decision, by declaring that the people of any State or Territory might withhold that protecting legislation, those "friendly police regulations," without which slavery could not exist. But this was, indeed, a "lame, illogical, evasive answer," which enabled Lincoln to "secure an advantage in the national relations of the contest which he held to the end."

Lincoln already had in mind the presidential nomination, and was fighting the present fight with an eye to that greater one in the near future.

Lincoln, in replying, agreed that "all the States have the right to do exactly as they please about all their domestic relations, including that of slavery." But he said that the proposition that slavery could not enter a new country without police regulations was historically false; and that the facts of the Dred Scott case itself showed that there was "vigor enough in slavery to plant itself in a new country even against unfriendly legislation." Beyond this issue of historical fact, Douglas had already taken and still dared to maintain a position which proved to be singularly ill chosen. The right to hold slaves as property in the Territories had lately, to the infinite joy of the South, been declared by the Supreme Court to be guaranteed by the Constitution; and now Douglas had the audacity to repeat that notion of his, so abhorrent to all friends of slavery,—that this invaluable right could be made practically worthless by unfriendly local legislation, or even by the negative hostility of withholding friendly legislation! From the moment when this deadly suggestion fell from his ingenious lips, the Southern Democracy turned upon him with vindictive hate and marked him for destruction. He had also given himself into the hands of his avowed and natural enemies. The doctrine, said Mr. Lincoln, is "no less than that a thing may lawfully be driven away from a place where it has a lawful right to be." "If you were elected members of the legislature, what would be the first thing you would have to do, before entering upon your duties? *Swear to support the Constitution of the United States*. Suppose you believe, as Judge Douglas does, that the Constitution of the United States guarantees to your neighbor the right to hold slaves in that Territory,—that they are his property,—how can you clear your oaths, unless you give him such legislation as is necessary to enable him to enjoy that property? What do you understand by supporting the Constitution of a State, or of the United States? Is it not to give such constitutional helps to the rights established by that

As it is with Bacon's essays, so it is with these speeches: the more attentively they are read the more striking appears the closeness of their texture both in logic and in language. Each sentence has its special errand.

Constitution as may be practically needed?... And what I say here will hold with still more force against the judge's doctrine of 'unfriendly legislation.' How could you, having sworn to support the Constitution, and believing it guaranteed the right to hold slaves in the Territories, assist in legislation *intended to defeat that right*?" "Is not Congress itself under obligation to give legislative support to any right that is established under the United States Constitution?" Upon what other principle do "many of us, who are opposed to slavery upon principle, give our acquiescence to a Fugitive Slave Law?" Does Douglas mean to say that a territorial legislature, "by passing unfriendly laws," can *"nullify a constitutional right?"* He put to Douglas the direct and embarrassing query: "If the slaveholding citizens of a United States Territory should need and demand congressional legislation for the protection of their slave property in such Territory, would you, as a member of Congress, vote for or against such legislation?" "Repeat that," cried Douglas, ostentatiously; "I want to answer that question." But he never composed his reply.

Another kindred question had already been put by Lincoln: "Can the people of a United States Territory, in any lawful way, against the wish of any citizen of the United States, exclude slavery from its limits, prior to the formation of a State Constitution?" Friends advised him not to force this, as it seemed against the immediate policy of the present campaign. But it was never his way to subordinate his own deliberate opinion to the opinions of advisers; and on this occasion he was merciless in pressing this question. A story has been very generally repeated that he told the protesters that, whatever might be the bearing on the senatorship, Douglas could not answer that question and be elected President of the United States in 1860. "I am killing larger game," he said; "the battle of 1860 is worth a hundred of this." A few legends of this kind are extant, which tend to indicate that Lincoln already had in mind the presidential nomination, and was fighting the present fight with an eye to that greater one in the near future. It is not easy to say how much credit should be given to such tales; they may not be wholly inventions, but a remark which is uttered with little thought may later easily take on a strong color in the light of subsequent developments.

In presenting the Republican side of the question Lincoln seemed to feel a duty beyond that of merely outarguing his opponent. He bore the weighty burden of a responsibility graver than personal success. He might prevail in the opinions of his fellow citizens; without this instant triumph he might so present his cause that the jury of posterity would declare that the truth lay with him; he might even convince both the present and the coming generations; and though achieving all these triumphs, he might still fall far short of the peculiar and exacting requirement of the occasion. For the winning of the senatorship was the insignificant part of what he had undertaken; his momentous charge was to maintain a grand moral crusade, to stimulate and to vindicate a great uprising in the cause of humanity and of justice. His full appreciation of this is entirely manifest in the tone of his speeches. They have an earnestness, a gravity, at times even a solemnity, unusual in such encounters in any era or before any audiences, but unprecedented "on the stump" before the uproarious gatherings of the West at that day. Repeatedly he stigmatized slavery as "a moral, a social, a political evil." Very impressively he denounced the positions of an opponent who "cared not whether slavery was voted down or voted up," who said that slavery was not to be differentiated from the many domestic institutions and daily affairs which civilized societies control by police regulations. He said that slavery could not be treated as "only equal to the cranberry laws of Indiana;" that slaves could not be put "upon a par with onions and potatoes;" that to Douglas he supposed that the institution really "looked small," but that a great proportion of the American people regarded slavery as "a vast moral evil." "The real issue in this controversy—the one pressing upon every mind—is the sentiment on the part of one class that looks upon the institution of slavery *as a wrong*, and of another class that does not look upon it as a wrong.... No man can logically say he does not care whether a wrong is voted up or voted down. He [Douglas] contends that whatever community wants slaves has a right to have them. So they have, if it is not a wrong. But if it is a wrong, he cannot say people have a right to do wrong. He says that, upon the score of equality, slaves should be allowed to go into a new Territory, like other property. This is strictly logical if there is no difference between it and other property.... But if you insist that one is wrong and the other right, there is no use to institute a comparison between right and wrong.... That is the real issue. That is the issue that will continue in this country when these poor tongues of Judge Douglas and myself shall be silent. It is the eternal struggle between these two principles, right and wrong, throughout the world. They are the two principles that have stood face to face from the beginning of time, and will ever continue to struggle. The one is the common right of humanity, and the other the divine right of kings. It is the same principle in whatever shape it develops itself. It is the same spirit that says: 'You work and toil and earn bread, and I'll eat it.'" "I ask you if it is not a false philosophy? Is it not a false statesmanship that undertakes to build up a system of policy upon the basis of caring nothing about *the very thing that everybody does care the most about?*"

We cannot leave these speeches without a word concerning their literary quality. In them we might have looked for vigor that would be a little uncouth, wit that would be often coarse, a logic generally sound but always clumsy,—in a word, tolerably good substance and very poor form. We are surprised, then, to find many and high excellences in art. As it is with Bacon's essays, so it is with these speeches: the more attentively they are read the more striking appears the closeness of their texture both in logic and in language. Clear thought is accurately expressed. Each sentence has its special errand, and each word its individual importance. There is never either too much or too little. The work is done with clean precision and no waste. Nowhere does one pause to seek a meaning or to recover a connection; and an effort to make out a syllabus shows that the most condensed statement has already been used. There are scintillations of wit and humor, but they are not very numerous. When Lincoln was urged to adopt a more popular style, he replied: "The occasion is too serious; the issues are too grave. I do not seek applause, or to amuse the people, but to convince them." This spirit was upon him from the beginning to the end. Had he been addressing a bench of judges, subject to a close limitation of

The truth which he had to sustain was so great that it was perfectly simple, and he had the good sense to utter it with appropriate simplicity.

minutes, he would have won credit by the combined economy and force which were displayed in these harangues to general assemblages. To speak of the lofty tone of these speeches comes dangerously near to the distasteful phraseology of extravagant laudation, than which nothing else can produce upon honest men a worse impression. Yet it is a truth visible to every reader that at the outset Lincoln raised the discussion to a very high plane, and held it there throughout. The truth which he had to sustain was so great that it was perfectly simple, and he had the good sense to utter it with appropriate simplicity. In no speech was there fervor or enthusiasm or rhetoric; he talked to the reason and the conscience of his auditors, not to their passions. Yet the depth of his feeling may be measured by the story that once in the canvass he said to a friend: "Sometimes, in the excitement of speaking, I seem to see the end of slavery. I feel that the time is soon coming when the sun shall shine, the rain fall, on no man who shall go forth to unrequited toil. How this will come, when it will come, by whom it will come, I cannot tell,—but that time will surely come."

It is just appreciation, and not extravagance, to say that the cheap and miserable little volume, now out of print, containing in bad newspaper type, "The Lincoln and Douglas Debates," holds some of the masterpieces of oratory of all ages and nations.

The immediate result of the campaign was the triumph of Douglas, who had certainly made not only a very able and brilliant but a splendidly gallant fight, with Republicans assailing him in front and Administrationists in rear. Lincoln was disappointed. His feelings had been so deeply engaged, he had worked so strenuously, and the result had been so much in doubt, that defeat was trying. But he bore it with his wonted resolute equanimity. He said that he felt "like the boy that stumped his toe,—'it hurt too bad to laugh, and he was too big to cry.'" In fact, there were encouraging elements. The popular vote stood, Republicans, 126,084; Douglas Democrats, 121,940; Lecompton Democrats, 5,091. But the apportionment of districts was such that the legislature contained a majority for Douglas. So the prestige of victory seemed separated from its fruits; for the nation, attentively watching this duel, saw that the new man had convinced upwards of four thousand voters more than had the great leader of the Democracy. Douglas is reported to have said that, during his sixteen years in Congress, he had found no man in the Senate whom he would not rather encounter in debate than Lincoln. If it was true that Lincoln was already dreaming of the presidency, he was a sufficiently shrewd politician to see that his prospects were greatly improved by this campaign. He had worked hard for what he had gained; he had been traveling incessantly to and fro and delivering speeches in unbroken succession during about one hundred of the hot days of the Western summer, and speeches not of a commonplace kind, but which severely taxed the speaker. After all was over, he was asked by the state committee to contribute to the campaign purse! He replied: "I am willing to pay according to my ability, but I am the poorest hand living to get others to pay. *I have been on expense* so long, without earning anything, that I am absolutely without money now for even household expenses. Still, if you can put in $250 for me,... I will allow it when you and I settle the private matter between us. This, with what I have already paid,... will exceed my subscription of $500. This, too, is exclusive of my ordinary expenses during the campaign, all of which being added to my loss of time and business bears pretty heavily upon one no better off than I am.... You are feeling badly; 'and this, too, shall pass away;' never fear."

The platform which, with such precision and painstaking, Lincoln had constructed for himself was made by him even more ample and more strong by a few speeches delivered in the interval between the close of this great campaign and his nomination by the Republicans for the presidency. In Ohio an important canvass for the governorship took place, and Douglas went there, and made speeches filled with allusions to Lincoln and the recent Illinois campaign. Even without this provocation Lincoln knew, by keen instinct, that where Douglas was, there he should be also. In no other way had he yet appeared to such advantage as in encountering "the Little Giant." To Ohio, accordingly, he hastened, and spoke at Columbus and at Cincinnati. To the citizens of the latter place he said: "This is the first time in my life that I have appeared before an audience in so great a city as this. I therefore make this appearance under some degree of embarrassment." There was little novelty in substance, but much in treatment. Thus, at Cincinnati, he imagined himself addressing Kentuckians, and showed them that their next nominee for the presidency ought to be his "distinguished friend, Judge Douglas;" for "in all that there is a difference between you and him, I understand he is sincerely for you, and more wisely for you than you are for yourselves." Through him alone pro-slavery men retained any hold upon the free States of the North; and in those States, "in every possible way he can, he constantly moulds the public opinion to your ends." Ingeniously but fairly he sketched Douglas as the most efficient among the pro-slavery leaders. Perhaps the clever and truthful picture may have led Mr. Greeley and some other gentlemen at the East to suspect that they had been inconsiderate in their choice between the Western rivals; and perhaps, also, Lincoln, while addressing imaginary Kentuckians, had before his inner eye some Eastern auditors. For at the time he did not know that his voice would ever be heard at any point nearer to their ears than the hall in which he then stood. Within a few weeks, however, this unlooked-for good fortune befell. In October, 1859, he was invited to speak in the following winter in New York. That the anti-slavery men of that city wished to test him by personal observation signified that his reputation was national, and that the highest aspirations were, therefore, not altogether presumptuous. He accepted gladly, and immediately began to prepare an address which probably cost him more labor than any other speech which he ever made. He found time, however, in December to make a journey through Kansas, where he delivered several speeches, which have not been preserved but are described as "repetitions of those previously made in Illinois." Lamon tells us that the journey was an "ovation," and that "wherever Lincoln went, he was met by vast assemblages of people." The population of this agricultural State was hardly in a condition to furnish "vast assemblages" at numerous points, but doubtless the visitor received gratifying assurance that upon this battle-ground of slavery and anti-slavery the winning party warmly appreciated his advocacy of their cause.

Probably the first impression made upon those auditors by the ungainly Westerner in his outlandish garb were not the same which they carried home with them a little later.

On Saturday, February 25, 1860, Lincoln arrived in New York. On Monday his hosts "found him dressed in a sleek and shining suit of new black, covered with very apparent creases and wrinkles, acquired by being packed too closely and too long in his little valise. He felt uneasy in his new clothes and a strange place." Certainly nothing in his previous experience had prepared him to meet with entire indifference an audience of metropolitan critics; indeed, had the surroundings been more familiar, he had enough at stake to tax his equanimity when William Cullen Bryant introduced him simply as "an eminent citizen of the West, hitherto known to you only by reputation." Probably the first impression made upon those auditors by the ungainly Westerner in his outlandish garb were not the same which they carried home with them a little later. The speech was so condensed that a sketch of it is not possible. Fortunately it had the excellent quality of steadily expanding in interest and improving to the end.

Of the Dred Scott case he cleverly said that the courts had decided it "*in a sort of way*;" but, after all, the decision was "mainly based upon a mistaken statement of fact,—the statement in the opinion that 'the right of property in a slave is distinctly and expressly affirmed in the Constitution.'"

In closing, he begged the Republicans, in behalf of peace and harmony, to "do nothing through passion and ill-temper;" but he immediately went on to show the antagonism between Republican opinion and Democratic opinion with a distinctness which left no hope of harmony, and very little hope of peace. To satisfy the Southerners, he said, we must "cease to call slavery *wrong*, and join them in calling it *right*. And this must be done thoroughly,—done in *acts* as well as in *words*.... We must arrest and return their fugitive slaves with greedy pleasure. We must pull down our free-state Constitutions.... If slavery is right, all words, acts, laws, and constitutions against it are themselves wrong, and should be silenced and swept away. If it is right, we cannot object to its nationality, its universality; if it is wrong, they cannot justly insist upon its extension, its enlargement. All they ask we could readily grant, if we thought slavery right; all we ask they could as readily grant, if they thought it wrong. Their thinking it right and our thinking it wrong is the precise fact upon which depends the whole controversy. Thinking it right, as they do, they are not to blame for desiring its full recognition, as being right; but thinking it wrong, as we do, can we yield to them?... Wrong as we think slavery is, we can yet afford to let it alone where it is, because that much is due to the necessity arising from its actual presence in the nation; but can we, while our votes will prevent it, allow it to spread into the national Territories, and to overrun us here in these free States? If our sense of duty forbids this ... let us be diverted by no sophistical contrivances, such as groping for some middle ground between the right and the wrong, vain as the search for a man who should be neither a living man nor a dead man; such as a policy of 'don't care' on a question about which all true men do care; such as Union appeals beseeching true Union men to yield to Disunionists, reversing the divine rule and calling not the sinners but the righteous to repentance."

The next morning the best newspapers gave full reports of the speech, with compliments. The columns of the "Evening Post" were generously declared to be "indefinitely elastic" for such utterances; and the "Tribune" expressed commendation wholly out of accord with the recent notions of its editor. The rough fellow from the crude West had made a powerful impression upon the cultivated gentlemen of the East.

From New York Lincoln went to Massachusetts, Rhode Island, New Hampshire, and Connecticut. In this last-named State he delivered speeches which are said to have contributed largely to the Republican success in the closely contested election then at hand. In Manchester it was noticed that "he did not abuse the South, the administration, or the Democrats, or indulge in any personalities, with the exception of a few hits at Douglas's notions."

He did what he could to give to the war a character far higher even than a war of patriotism, for he extended its meaning far beyond the age and the country of its occurrence, and made of it, not a war for the United States alone, but a war for humanity, a war for ages and peoples yet to come.

These speeches of 1858, 1859, and 1860 have a very great value as contributions to history. During that period every dweller in the United States was hotly concerned about this absorbing question of slavery, advancing his own views, weighing or encountering the arguments of others, quarreling, perhaps, with his oldest friends and his nearest kindred,—for about this matter men easily quarreled and rarely compromised. Every man who fancied that he could speak in public got upon some platform in city, town, or village, and secured an audience by his topic if not by his ability; every one who thought that he could write found some way to print what he had to say upon a subject of which readers never tired; and for whatever purpose two or three men were gathered together, they were not likely to separate without a few words about North and

South, pro-slavery and anti-slavery. Never was any matter more harried and ransacked by disputation. Now to all the speaking and writing of the Republicans Lincoln's condensed speeches were what a syllabus is to an elaborate discourse, what a lawyer's brief is to his verbal argument. Perhaps they may better be likened to an anti-slavery gospel; as the New Testament is supposed to cover the whole ground of Christian doctrines and Christian ethics, so that theologians and preachers innumerable have only been able to make elaborations or glosses upon the original text, so Lincoln's speeches contain the whole basis of the anti-slavery cause as maintained by the Republican party. They also set forth a considerable part of the Southern position, doubtless as fairly as the machinations of the Devil are set forth in Holy Writ. They only rather gingerly refrain from speaking of the small body of ultra-Abolitionists,— for while Lincoln was far from agreeing with these zealots, he felt that it was undesirable to widen by any excavation upon his side the chasm between them and the Republicans. So the fact is that the whole doctrine of Republicanism, as it existed during the political campaign which resulted in the election of Lincoln, also all the historical facts supporting that doctrine, were clearly and accurately stated in these speeches. Specific points were more elaborated by other persons; but every seed was to be found in this granary.

This being the case, it is worth noticing that both Lincoln and Douglas confined their disputation closely to the slavery question. Disunion and secession were words familiar in every ear, yet Lincoln referred to these things only twice or thrice, and incidentally, while Douglas ignored them. This fact is fraught with meaning. American writers and American readers have always met upon the tacit understanding that the Union was the chief cause of, and the best justification for, the war. An age may come when historians, treating our history as we treat that of Greece, stirred by no emotion at the sight of the "Stars and Stripes," moved by no patriotism at the name of the United States of America, will seek a deeper philosophy to explain this obstinate, bloody, costly struggle. Such writers may say that a rich, civilized multitude of human beings, possessors of the quarter of a continent, believing it best for their interests to set up an independent government for themselves, fell back upon the right of revolution, though they chose not to call it by that name. Now, even if it be possible to go so far as to say that every nation has always a right to preserve by force, if it can, its own integrity, certainly it cannot be stated as a further truth that no portion of a nation can ever be justified in endeavoring to obtain an independent national existence; no citizen of this country can admit this, but must say that such an endeavor is justifiable or not justifiable according as its cause and basis are right or wrong. Far down, then, at the very bottom lay the question whether the Southerners had a sufficient cause upon which to base a revolution. Now this question was hardly conclusively answered by the perfectly true statement that the North had not interfered with Southern rights. Southerners might admit this, and still believe that their welfare could be best subserved by a government wholly their own. So the very bottom question of all still remained: Was the South endeavoring to establish a government of its own for a justifiable reason and a right purpose? Now the avowed purpose was to establish on an enduring foundation a permanent slave empire; and the declared reason was, that slavery was not safe within the Union. Underneath the question of the Union therefore lay, logically, the question of slavery.

Lincoln and the other Republican leaders said that, if slavery extension was prevented, then slavery was in the way of extinction. If the assertion was true, it pretty clearly followed that the South could retain slavery only by independence and a complete imperial control within the limits of its own homogeneous nationality; for undeniably the preponderant Northern mass was becoming firmly resolved that slavery should not be extended, however it might be tolerated within its present limits. So still, by anti-slavery statement itself, the ultimate question was: whether or not the preservation of slavery was a right and sufficient cause or purpose for establishing an independent nationality. Lincoln, therefore, went direct to the logical heart of the contention, when he said that the real dispute was whether slavery was a right thing or a wrong thing. If slavery was a right thing, a Union conducted upon a policy which was believed to doom it to "ultimate extinction" was not a right thing. But if slavery was a wrong thing, a revolution undertaken with the purpose of making it perpetual was also a wrong thing. Therefore, from beginning to end, Lincoln talked about slavery. By so doing he did what he could to give to the war a character far higher even than a war of patriotism, for he extended its meaning far beyond the age and the country of its occurrence, and made of it, not a war for the United States alone, but a war for humanity, a war for ages and peoples yet to come. In like manner, he himself also gained the right to be regarded as much more than a great party leader, even more than a great patriot; for he became a champion of mankind and the defender of the chief right of man. I do not mean to say that he saw these things in this light at the moment, or that he accurately formulated the precise relationship and fundamental significance of all that was then in process of saying and doing. Time must elapse, and distance must enable one to get a comprehensive view, before the philosophy of an era like that of the civil war becomes intelligible. But the philosophy is not the less correct because those who were framing it piece by piece did not at any one moment project before their mental vision the whole in its finished proportions and relationship.

CHAPTER VI

ELECTION

"Wigwam," Chicago

*"…I beg that you will not give it further mention.
I do not think I am fit for the presidency."*

Mr. J.W. Fell, a leading citizen of Illinois, says that after the debates of 1858 he urged Lincoln to seek the Republican nomination for the presidency in 1860. Lincoln, however, replied curtly that men like Seward and Chase were entitled to take precedence, and that no such "good luck" was in store for him. In March, 1859, he wrote to another person: "In regard to the other matter that you speak of, I beg that you will not give it further mention. I do not think I am fit for the presidency." He said the same to the editor of the "Central Illinois Gazette;" but this gentleman "brought him out in the issue of May 4," and "thence the movement spread rapidly and strongly." In the winter of 1859-60 sundry "intimate friends," active politicians of Illinois, pressed him to consent to be mentioned as a candidate. He considered the matter over night and then gave them the desired permission, at the same time saying that he would not accept the vice-presidency.

Being now fairly started in the race, he used all his well-known skill as a politician to forward his campaign, though nothing derogatory is to be inferred from these words as to his conduct or methods. February 9, 1860, he wrote to Mr. Judd: "I am not in a position where it would hurt much for me not to be nominated on the national ticket; but I am where it would hurt some for me not to get the Illinois delegates.... Can you help me a little in this matter at your end of the vineyard?" This point of the allegiance of his own State was soon made right. The Republican State Convention met in the "Wigwam" at Decatur, May 9 and 10, 1860. Governor Oglesby, who presided, suggested that a distinguished citizen, whom Illinois delighted to honor, was present, and that he should be invited to a place on the stand; and at once, amid a tumult of applause, Lincoln was lifted over the heads of the crowd to the platform. John Hanks then theatrically entered, bearing a couple of fence rails, and a flag with the legend that they were from a "lot made by Abraham Lincoln and John Hanks in the Sangamon Bottom, in the year 1830." The sympathetic roar rose again. Then Lincoln made a "speech," appropriate to the occasion. At last, attention was given to business, and the convention resolved that Abraham Lincoln was the first choice of the Republican party of Illinois for the presidency, and instructed their delegates to the nominating convention "to use all honorable means to secure his nomination, and to cast the vote of the State as a unit for him."

With the opening of the spring of 1860 the several parties began the campaign in earnest. The Democratic Convention met first, at Charleston, April 23; and immediately the line of disruption opened. Upon the one side stood Douglas, with the moderate men and nearly all the Northern delegates, while against him were the advocates of extreme Southern doctrines, supported by the administration and by most of the delegates from the "Cotton States." The majority of the committee appointed to draft the platform were anti-Douglas men; but their report was rejected, and that offered by the pro-Douglas minority was substituted, 165 yeas to 138 nays. Thereupon the delegations of Alabama, Mississippi, Florida, and Texas, and sundry delegates from other States, withdrew from the convention, taking away 45 votes out of a total of

The Republican party was laden with the burden of an immense responsibility, and the men who did its thinking could not reasonably feel certain that rail-splitting was an altogether satisfactory training for the leader in such an era as was now at hand.

303. Those who remained declared the vote of two thirds of a full convention, *i.e.*, 202 votes, to be necessary for a choice. Then during three days fifty-seven ballots were cast, Douglas being always far in the lead, but never polling more than 152½ votes. At last, on May 3, an adjournment was had until June 18, at Baltimore. At this second meeting contesting delegations appeared, and the decisions were uniformly in favor of the Douglas men, which provoked another secession of the extremist Southern men. A ballot showed 173½ votes for Douglas out of a total of 191½; the total was less than two thirds of the full number of the original convention, and therefore it was decided that any person receiving two thirds of the votes cast by the delegates present should be deemed the nominee. The next ballot gave Douglass 181½. Herschel V. Johnson of Georgia was nominated for vice-president.

On June 28, also at Baltimore, there came together a collection composed of original seceders at Charleston, and of some who had been rejected and others who had seceded at Baltimore. Very few Northern men were present, and the body in fact represented the Southern wing of the Democracy. Having, like its competitor, the merit of knowing its own mind, it promptly nominated John C. Breckenridge of Kentucky and Joseph Lane of Oregon, and adopted the radical platform which had been reported at Charleston.

These doings opened, so that it could never be closed, that seam of which the thread had long been visible athwart the surface of the old Democratic party. The great record of discipline and of triumph, which the party had made when united beneath the dominion of imperious leaders, was over, and forever. Those questions which Lincoln obstinately and against advice had insisted upon pushing in 1858 had forced this disastrous development of irreconcilable differences. The answers, which Douglas could not shirk, had alienated the most implacable of men, the dictators of the Southern Democracy. His "looking-both-ways" theory would not fit with their policy, and their policy was and must be immutable; modification was in itself defeat. On the other hand, what he said constituted the doctrine to which the mass of the Northern Democracy firmly

Lincoln plainly asserted a policy which the Abolitionists equally plainly condemned.

held. So now, although Republicans admitted that it was "morally certain" that the Democratic party, holding together, could carry the election, yet these men from the Cotton States could not take victory and Douglas together. It had actually come to this, that, in spite of all that Douglas had done for the slaveholders, they now marked him for destruction at any cost. Many also believe that they had another motive; that they had matured their plans for secession; and that they did not mean to have the scheme disturbed or postponed by an ostensibly Democratic triumph in the shape of the election of Douglas.

In May the convention of the Constitutional Union party met, also at Baltimore. This organization was a sudden outgrowth designed only to meet the present emergency. Its whole political doctrine lay in the opening words of the one resolution which constituted its platform: "That it is both the part of patriotism and of duty to recognize no political principle other than the Constitution of the country, the union of the States, and the enforcement of the laws." This party gathered nearly all the peaceable elements of the community; it assumed a deprecatory attitude between angry contestants, and of course received the abuse and contempt of both; it was devoid of combative force, yet had some numerical strength. The Republicans especially mocked at these "trimmers," as if their only platform was moral cowardice, which, however, was an unfair statement of their position. The party died, of necessity, upon the day when Lincoln was elected, and its members were then distributed between the Republicans, the Secessionists, and the Copperheads. John Bell of Tennessee, the candidate for the presidency, joined the Confederacy; Edward Everett of Massachusetts, the candidate for the vice-presidency, became a Republican. The party never had a hope of electing its men; but its existence increased the chance of throwing the election into Congress; and this hope inspired exertions far beyond what its own prospects warranted.

On May 16 the Republican Convention came together at Chicago, where the great "Wigwam" had been built to hold 10,000 persons. The intense interest with which its action was watched indicated the popular belief that probably it would name the next President of the United States. Many candidates were named, chiefly Seward, Lincoln, Chase, Cameron, Edward Bates of Missouri, and William L. Dayton of New Jersey. Thurlow Weed was Seward's lieutenant. Horace Greeley, chiefly bent upon the defeat of Seward, would have liked to achieve it by the success of Bates. David Davis, aided by Judge Logan and a band of personal friends from Illinois, was manager for Lincoln. Primarily the contest lay between Seward and Lincoln, and only a dead-lock between these two could give a chance to some one of the others. But Seward's friends hoped, and Lincoln's friends dreaded, that the New Yorker might win by a rush on the first ballot. George Ashmun of Massachusetts presided. With little discussion a platform was adopted, long and ill-written, overloaded with adjectives and rhetoric, sacrificing dignity to the supreme pleasure of abusing the Democracy, but honest in stating Republican doctrines, and clearly displaying the temper of an earnest, aggressive party, hot for the fight and confident of victory. The vote of acceptance was greeted with such a cheering that "a herd of buffaloes or lions could not have made a more tremendous roaring."

The details of the brief but sharp contest for the nomination are not altogether gratifying. The partisans of Seward set about winning votes by much parading in the streets with banners and music, and by out-yelling all competitors within the walls of the convention. For this intelligent purpose they had engaged Tom Hyer, the prize fighter, with a gang of roughs, to hold possession of the Wigwam, and to howl illimitably at appropriate moments. But they had undertaken a difficult task in trying to outdo the great West, in one of its own cities, at a game of this kind. The Lincoln leaders in their turn secured a couple of stentorian yellers (one of them a Democrat), instructed them carefully, and then filled the Wigwam full actually at daybreak, while the Seward men were marching; so in the next yelling match the West won magnificently. How great was the real efficiency of these tactics in affecting the choice of the ruler of a great nation commonly accounted intelligent, it is difficult to say with accuracy; but it is certain that the expert managers spared no pains about this scenic business of "enthusiasm."

Meanwhile other work, entirely quiet, was being done elsewhere. The objection to Seward was that he was too radical, too far in advance of the party. The Bates following were pushing their candidate as a moderate man, who would be acceptable to "Union men." But Bates's chance was small, and any tendency towards a moderate candidate was likely to carry his friends to Lincoln rather than to Seward; for Lincoln was generally supposed, however erroneously, to be more remote from Abolitionism than Seward was. To counteract this, a Seward delegate telegraphed to the Bates men at St. Louis that Lincoln was as radical as Seward. Lincoln, at Springfield, saw this dispatch, and at once wrote a message to David Davis: "Lincoln agrees with Seward in his irrepressible-conflict idea, and in Negro Equality; but he is opposed to Seward's Higher Law. *Make no contracts that will bind me.*" He underscored the

last sentence; but when his managers saw it, they recognized that such
independence did not accord with the situation, and so they set it aside.

The first vote was:—

Whole number 465

Necessary for choice 233

William H. Seward of New York 173½

Abraham Lincoln of Illinois 102

Simon Cameron of Pennsylvania 50½

Salmon P. Chase of Ohio 49

Edward Bates of Missouri 48

William L. Dayton of New Jersey 14

John McLean of Ohio 12

Jacob Collamer of Vermont 10

Scattering 6

The fact was, and Lincoln's friends perfectly understood it, that Cameron
held that peculiar kind of power which gave him no real prospect of success, yet
had a considerable salable value. Could they refrain from trying the market?
They asked the owners of the 50½ Cameron votes what was their price. The
owners said: The Treasury Department. Lincoln's friends declared this
extravagant. Then they all chaffered. Finally Cameron's men took a place in the
cabinet, without further specification. Lamon says that another smaller contract
was made with the friends of Caleb B. Smith. Then the Lincoln managers
rested in a pleasing sense of security.

The second ballot showed slight changes:—

Seward 184½

Lincoln 181

Cameron 2

Chase 42½

Bates 5

Dayton 10

McLean 8

Scattering 2

Upon the third ballot delivery was made of what Mr. Davis had bought. That epidemic foreknowledge, which sometimes so unaccountably foreruns an event, told the convention that the decision was at hand. A dead silence reigned save for the click of the telegraphic instruments and the low scratching of hundreds of pencils checking off the votes as the roll was called. Those who were keeping the tally saw that it stood:—

Seward	180
Lincoln	231½
Chase	24½
Bates	22
Dayton	1
McLean	5
Scattering	1

Cameron was out of the race; Lincoln was within 1½ votes of the goal. Before the count could be announced, a delegate from Ohio transferred four votes to Lincoln. This settled the matter; and then other delegations followed, till Lincoln's score rose to 354. At once the "enthusiasm" of 10,000 men again reduced to insignificance a "herd of buffaloes or lions." When at last quiet was restored, William M. Evarts, who had led for Seward, offered the usual motion to make the nomination of Abraham Lincoln unanimous. It was done. Again the "tremendous roaring" arose. Later in the day the convention nominated Hannibal Hamlin of Maine, on the second ballot, by 367 votes, for the vice-presidency. Then for many hours, till exhaustion brought rest, Chicago was given over to the wonted follies; cannon boomed, music resounded, and streets and barrooms were filled with the howling and drinking crowds of the intelligent promoters of one of the great moral crusades of the human race.

Lamon says that the committee deputed to wait upon Lincoln at Springfield found him "sad and dejected. The reaction from excessive joy to deep despondency—a process peculiar to his constitution—had already set in." His remarks to these gentlemen were brief and colorless. His letter afterward was little more than a simple acceptance of the platform.

·   ·   ·   ·   ·   ·   ·   ·   ·   ·

Since white men first landed on this continent, the selection of Washington to lead the army of the Revolution is the only event to be compared in good fortune with this nomination of Abraham Lincoln. Yet the convention deserved no credit for its action. It did not know the true ratio between Seward and Lincoln, which only the future was to make plain. By all that it did know, it ought to have given the honor to Seward, who merited it by the high offices which he had held with distinction and without blemish, by the leadership which he had acquired in the party through long-continued constancy and courage, by the force and clearness with which he had maintained its principles, by his experience and supposed natural aptitude in the higher walks of statesmanship. Yet actually by reason of these very qualifications it was now admitted that the all-important "October States" of Indiana and Pennsylvania could not be carried by the Republicans if Seward were nominated; while Greeley, sitting in the convention as a substitute for a delegate from Oregon, cast as much of the weight of New York as he could lift into the anti-Seward scale. In plain fact, the convention, by its choice, paid no compliment either to Lincoln or to the voters of the party. They took him because he was "available," and the reason that he was "available" lay not in any popular appreciation of his merits, but in the contrary truth,—that the mass of people could place no intelligent estimate upon him at all, either for good or for ill. Outside of Illinois a few men, who had studied his speeches, esteemed him an able man in debate; more had a vague notion of him as an effective stump speaker of the West; far the greatest number had to find out about him. In a word, Mr. Lincoln gained the nomination because Mr. Seward had been "too conspicuous," whereas he himself was so little known that it was possible for Wendell Phillips to inquire indignantly: "Who is this huckster in politics? Who is this county court advocate?" For these singular reasons he was the most "available" candidate who could be offered before the citizens of the United States!

It cannot be said that the nomination was received with much satisfaction. "Honest old Abe the rail-splitter!" might sound well in the ear of the masses;

but the Republican party was laden with the burden of an immense responsibility, and the men who did its thinking could not reasonably feel certain that rail-splitting was an altogether satisfactory training for the leader in such an era as was now at hand. Nevertheless, nearly all came to the work of the campaign with as much zeal as if they had surely known the full value of their candidate. Shutting their minds against doubts, they made the most spirited and energetic canvass which has ever taken place in the country. The organization of the "Wide-Awake" clubs was an effective success. None who saw will ever forget the spectacle presented by these processions wherein many thousands of men, singing the campaign songs, clad in uniform capes of red or white oil-cloth, each with a flaming torch or a colored lantern, marched nightly in every city and town of the North, in apparently endless numbers and with military precision, making the streets a brilliant river of variously tinted flame. Torchlight parades have become mere conventional affairs since those days, when there was a spirit in them which nothing has ever stirred more lately. They were a good preparation for the more serious marching and severer drill which were soon to come, though the Republicans scoffed at all anticipations of such a future, and sneered at the timid ones who croaked of war and bloodshed.

Almost from the beginning it was highly probable that the Republicans would win, and it was substantially certain that none of their competitors could do so. The only contrary chance was that no election might be made by the people, and that it might be thrown into Congress. Douglas with his wonted spirit made a vigorous fight, traveling to and fro, speaking constantly in the North and a few times in the South, but defiant rather than conciliatory in tone. He did not show one whit the less energy because it was obvious that he waged a contest without hope. If there were any road to Democratic success, which it now seems that there was not, it lay in uniting the sundered party. An attempt was made to arrange that whichever Democratic candidate should ultimately display the greater strength should receive the full support of the party. Projects for a fusion ticket met with some success in New York. In Pennsylvania like schemes were imperfectly successful. In other Northern States they were received with scant favor. Except some followers of Bell and Everett, men were in no temper for compromise. At the South fusion was not even attempted; the Breckenridge men would not hear of it; the voters in that section were controlled by leaders, and these leaders probably had a very distinct policy, which would be seriously interfered with by the triumph of the Douglas ticket.

The chief anxiety of Lincoln and the Republican leaders was lest some voters, who disagreed with them only on less important issues, might stay away from the polls. All the platforms, except that of the Constitutional Union party, touched upon other topics besides the question of slavery in the Territories; the tariff, native Americanism, acquisition of Cuba, a transcontinental railway, public lands, internal improvements, all found mention. The Know-Nothing party still by occasional twitchings showed that life had not quite taken flight, and endeavors were made to induce Lincoln to express his views. But he evaded it. For above all else he wished to avoid the stirring of any dissension upon side issues or minor points; his hope was to see all opponents of the extension of slavery put aside for a while all other matters, refrain from discussing troublesome details, and unite for the one broad end of putting slavery where "the fathers" had left it, so that the "public mind should rest in the belief that it

His career as president was made infinitely more difficult as well as greatly more creditable to him by reason of the very fact that he was not *the choice of the American people, but of less than half of them.*

was in the way of ultimate extinction." He felt it to be fair and right that he should receive the votes of all anti-slavery men; and ultimately he did, with the exception only of the thorough-going Abolitionists.

It was not so very long since he had spoken of the Abolitionist leaders as "friends;" but they did not reciprocate the feeling, nor indeed could reasonably be expected to do so, or to vote the Republican ticket. They were even less willing to vote it with Lincoln at the head of it than if Seward had been there. But Republicanism itself under any leader was distinctly at odds with their views; for when they said "*abolition*" they meant accurately what they said, and abolition certainly was impossible under the Constitution. The Republicans, and Lincoln personally, with equal directness acknowledged the supremacy of the Constitution. Lincoln, therefore, plainly asserted a policy which the Abolitionists equally plainly condemned. In their eyes, to be a party to a contract maintaining slavery throughout a third of a continent was only a trifle less criminal than aiding to extend it over another third. Yet it should be said that the Abolitionists were not all of one mind, and some voted the Republican ticket as being at least a step in the right direction. Joshua R. Giddings was a member of the Republican Convention which nominated Lincoln. But Wendell Phillips, always an extremist among extremists, published an article entitled "Abraham Lincoln, the Slave-hound of Illinois," whereof the keynote was struck in this introductory sentence: "We gibbet a Northern hound to-day, side by side with the infamous Mason of Virginia." Mr. Garrison, a man of far larger and sounder intellectual powers than belonged to Phillips, did not fancy this sort of diatribe, though five months earlier he had accused the Republican party of "slavish subserviency to the Union," and declared it to be "still insanely engaged in glorifying the Union and pledging itself to frown upon all attempts to dissolve it." Undeniably men who held these views could not honestly vote for Mr. Lincoln.

The popular vote and the electoral vote were as follows:—

STATES.	POPULAR VOTE.				ELECTORAL VOTE.			
	Abraham Lincoln, Illinois.	Stephen A. Douglas, Illinois.	John C. Breckenridge, Kentucky.	John Bell, Tennessee.	Lincoln.	Douglas.	Breckenridge.	Bell.
Maine	62,811	26,693	6,368	2,046	8	—	—	—
New Hampshire	37,519	25,881	2,112	441	5	—	—	—
Vermont	33,808	6,849	218	1,969	5	—	—	—
Massachusetts	106,533	34,372	5,939	22,231	13	—	—	—
Rhode Island	12,244	7,707†	—	—	4	—	—	—
Connecticut	43,792	15,522	14,641	3,291	6	—	—	—
New York	362,646	312,510†	—	—	35	—	—	—
New Jersey	58,324	62,801†	—	—	4	3	—	—
Pennsylvania	268,030	16,765	178,871†	12,776	27	—	—	—
Delaware	3,815	1,023	7,337	3,864	—	—	3	—
Maryland	2,294	5,966	42,482	41,760	—	—	8	—
Virginia	1,929	16,290	74,323	74,681	—	—	—	15
North Carolina	—	2,701	48,539	44,990	—	—	10	—
South Carolina*	—	—	—	—	—	—	8	—
Georgia	—	11,590	51,889	42,886	—	—	10	—
Florida	—	367	8,543	5,437	—	—	3	—
Alabama	—	13,651	48,831	27,875	—	—	9	—
Mississippi	—	3,283	40,797	25,040	—	—	7	—
Louisiana	—	7,625	22,861	20,204	—	—	6	—
Texas	—	—	47,548	15,438†	—	—	4	—
Arkansas	—	5,227	28,732	20,094	—	—	4	—
Missouri	17,028	58,801	31,317	58,372	—	9	—	—
Tennessee	—	11,350	64,709	69,274	—	—	—	12
Kentucky	1,364	25,651	53,143	66,058	—	—	—	12
Ohio	231,610	187,232	11,405	12,194	23	—	—	—
Michigan	88,480	65,057	805	405	6	—	—	—
Indiana	139,033	115,509	12,295	5,306	13	—	—	—
Illinois	172,161	160,215	2,404	4,913	11	—	—	—
Wisconsin	86,110	65,021	888	161	5	—	—	—
Minnesota	22,069	11,920	748	62	4	—	—	—
Iowa	70,409	55,111	1,048	1,763	4	—	—	—
California	39,173	38,516	34,334	6,817	4	—	—	—
Oregon	5,270	3,951	5,006	183	3	—	—	—
Totals	1,866,452	1,375,157	847,953	590,631	180	12	72	39

* By legislature.　　　　† Fusion electoral tickets.

Messrs. Nicolay and Hay say that Lincoln was the "indisputable choice of the American people," and by way of sustaining the statement say that, if the "whole voting strength of the three opposing parties had been united upon a single candidate, Lincoln would nevertheless have been chosen with only a trifling diminution of his electoral majority." It might be better to say that Lincoln was the "indisputable choice" of the electoral college. The "American people" fell enormously short of showing a majority in his favor. His career as president was made infinitely more difficult as well as greatly more creditable to him by reason of the very fact that he was *not* the choice of the American people, but of less than half of them,—and this, too, even if the Confederate States be excluded from the computation.

The election of Lincoln was "hailed with delight" by the extremists in South Carolina; for it signified secession, and the underlying and real desire of these people was secession, and not either compromise or postponement.

CHAPTER VII

INTERREGNUM

The White House

"*My course is as plain as a turnpike
road. It is marked out by the Constitution.
I am in no doubt which way to go.*"

For a while now the people of the Northern States were compelled passively to behold a spectacle which they could not easily reconcile with the theory of the supreme excellence and wisdom of their system of government. Abraham Lincoln was chosen President of the United States November 6, 1860; he was to be inaugurated March 4, 1861. During the intervening four months the government must be conducted by a chief whose political creed was condemned by an overwhelming majority of the nation. The situation was as unfair for Mr. Buchanan as it was hurtful for the people. As head of a republic, or, in the more popular phrase, as the chief "servant of the people," he must respect the popular will, yet he could not now administer the public business according to that will without being untrue to all his own convictions, and repudiating all his trusted counselors. In a situation so intrinsically false efficient government was impossible, no matter what was the strength or weakness of the hand at the helm. Therefore there was every reason for displacing Buchanan from control of the national affairs in the autumn, and every reason against continuing him in that control through the winter; yet the law of the land ordained the latter course. It seemed neither sensible nor even safe. During this doleful period all descriptions of him agree: he seemed, says Chittenden, "shaken in body and uncertain in mind,... an old man worn out by worry;" while the Southerners also declared him as "incapable of purpose as a child." To the like purport spoke nearly all who saw him.

During the same time Lincoln's position was equally absurd and more trying. After the lapse of four months he was, by the brief ceremony of an hour, to become the leader of a great nation under an exceptionally awful responsibility; but during those four months he could play no other part than simply to watch, in utter powerlessness, the swift succession of crowding events, which all were tending to make his administration of the government difficult, or even impossible. Throughout all this long time, the third part of a year, which statutes scarcely less venerable than the Constitution itself freely presented to the disunion leaders, they safely completed their civil and military organization, while the Northerners, under a ruler whom they had discredited, but of whom they could not get rid, were paralyzed for all purposes of counter preparation.

As a trifling compensation for its existence this costly interregnum presents to later generations a curious spectacle. A volume might be made of the public utterances put forth in that time by men of familiar names and more or less high repute, and it would show many of them in most strange and unexpected characters, so entirely out of keeping with the years which they had lived before, and the years which they were to live afterward, that the reader would gaze in hopeless bewilderment. In the "solid" South, so soon to be a great rebelling unit, he would find perhaps half of the people opposed to disunion; in the North he would hear everywhere words of compromise and concession, while coercion would be mentioned only to be denounced. If these four months were useful in bringing the men of the North to the fighting point, on the other hand they gave an indispensable opportunity for proselyting, by whirl and excitement,

Though the popular discontent was far short of the revolutionary point, yet individuals, one after another, yielded to that sympathetic, emotional instinct which tempts each man to fall in with the big procession.

great numbers at the South. Even in the autumn of 1860 and in the Gulf States secession was still so much the scheme of leaders that there was no popular preponderance in favor of disunion doctrines. In evidence of this are the responses of governors to a circular letter of Governor Gist of South Carolina, addressed to them October 5, 1860, and seeking information as to the feeling among the people. From North Carolina, Louisiana, Georgia, and Alabama came replies that secession was not likely to be favorably received. Mississippi was non-committal. Louisiana, Georgia, and Alabama desired a convention of the discontented States, and might be influenced by its action. North Carolina, Louisiana, and Alabama would oppose forcible coercion of a seceding State. Florida alone was rhetorically belligerent. These reports were discouraging in the ears of the extremist governor; but against them he could set the fact that the disunionists had the advantage of being the aggressive, propagandist body, homogeneous, and pursuing an accurate policy in entire concert. They were willing to take any amount of pains to manipulate and control the election of delegates and the formal action of conventions, and in all cases except that of Texas the question was conclusively passed upon by conventions. By every means they "fired the Southern heart," which was notoriously combustible; they stirred up a great tumult of sentiment; they made thunderous speeches; they kept distinguished emissaries moving to and fro; they celebrated each success with an uproar of cannonading, with bonfires, illuminations, and processions; they appealed to those chivalrous virtues supposed to be peculiar to Southerners; they preached devotion to the State, love of the state flag, generous

By the light that was in him Mr. Buchanan was a Unionist, but it was a sadly false and flickering light, and beneath its feeble illumination his steps staggered woefully.

loyalty to sister slave-communities; sometimes they used insult, abuse, and intimidation; occasionally they argued seductively. Thus Mr. Cobb's assertion, that "we can make better terms out of the Union than in it," was, in the opinion of Alexander H. Stephens, the chief influence which carried Georgia out of the Union. In the main, however, it was the principle of state sovereignty and state patriotism which proved the one entirely trustworthy influence to bring over the reluctant. "I abhor disunion, but I go with my State," was the common saying; and the States were under skillful and resolute leadership. So, though the popular discontent was far short of the revolutionary point, yet individuals, one after another, yielded to that sympathetic, emotional instinct which tempts each man to fall in with the big procession. In this way it was that during the Buchanan interregnum the people of the Gulf States became genuinely fused in rebellion.

It is not correct to say that the election of Lincoln was the cause of the Rebellion; it was rather the signal. To the Southern leaders, it was the striking of the appointed hour. His defeat would have meant only postponement. South Carolina led the way. On December 17, 1860, her convention came together, the Palmetto flag waving over its chamber of conference, and on December 20 it issued its "Ordinance." This declared that the Ordinance of May 23, 1788, ratifying the Constitution, is "hereby repealed," and the "Union now subsisting between South Carolina and other States, under the name of the United States of America, is hereby dissolved." A Declaration of Causes said that South Carolina had "resumed her position among the nations of the world as a separate and independent State." The language used was appropriate for the revocation of a power of attorney. The people hailed this action with noisy joy, unaccompanied by any regret or solemnity at the severance of the old relationship. The newspapers at once began to publish "Foreign News" from the other States. The new governor, Pickens, a fiery Secessionist, and described as one "born insensible to fear,"—presumably the condition of most persons at that early period of existence,—had already suggested to Mr. Buchanan the impropriety of reinforcing the national garrisons in the forts in Charleston harbor. He now accredited to the President three commissioners to treat with him for the delivery of the "forts, magazines, lighthouses, and other real estate, with their appurtenances, in the limits of South Carolina; and also for an apportionment of the public debt, and for a division of all other property held by the government of the United States as agent of the Confederate States of which South Carolina was recently a member." This position, as of the dissolution of a copartnership, or the revocation of an agency, and an accounting of debts and assets, was at least simple; and by way of expediting it an appraisal of the "real estate" and "appurtenances" within the state limits had been made by the state government. Meanwhile there was in the harbor of Charleston a sort of armed truce, which might at any moment break into war. Major Anderson in Fort Moultrie, and the state commander in the city, watched each other like two suspicious animals, neither sure when the other will spring. In short, in all the overt acts, the demeanor and the language of this excitable State, there was such insolence, besides hostility, that her emissaries must have been surprised at the urbane courtesy with which they were received, even by a President of Mr. Buchanan's views.

After the secession of South Carolina the other Gulf States hesitated briefly. Mississippi followed first; her convention assembled January 7, 1861, and on January 9 passed the ordinance, 84 yeas to 15 nays, subsequently making the vote unanimous. The Florida convention met January 3, and on January 10 decreed the State to be "a sovereign and independent nation," 62 yeas to 7 nays. The Alabama convention passed its ordinance on January 11 by 61 yeas to 39 nays; the President announced that the idea of reconstruction must be forever "dismissed." Yet the northern part of the State appeared to be substantially anti-secession. In Georgia the Secessionists doubted whether they could control a convention, yet felt obliged to call one. Toombs, Cobb, and Iverson labored with tireless zeal throughout the State; but in spite of all their proselyting, Unionist feeling ran high and debate was hot. The members from the southern part of the State ventured to menace and dragoon those from the northern part, who were largely Unionists. The latter retorted angrily; a schism and personal collisions were narrowly avoided. Alexander H. Stephens spoke for the Union with a warmth and logic not surpassed by anything that was said at the North. He and Herschel V. Johnson both voted against secession; yet, on January 18, when the vote was taken, it showed 208 yeas against 89 nays. On January 26 Louisiana followed, the vote of the convention being 113 yeas to 17 nays; but it refused to submit the ordinance to the people for ratification. The action of Texas, the only other State which seceded prior to the inauguration of Lincoln, was delayed until February 1. There Governor Houston was opposing secession with such vigor as remained to a broken old man, whereby he provoked Senator Iverson to utter the threat of assassination: "Some Texan Brutus may arise to rid his country of this old hoary-headed traitor." But in the convention, when it came to voting, the yeas were 166, the nays only 7.

By the light that was in him Mr. Buchanan was a Unionist, but it was a sadly false and flickering light, and beneath its feeble illumination his steps staggered woefully. For two months he diverged little from the path which the Secessionist leaders would have marked out for him, had they controlled his movements. At the time of the election his cabinet was:—

Lewis Cass of Michigan, secretary of state.

Howell Cobb of Georgia, secretary of the treasury.

John B. Floyd of Virginia, secretary of war.

Isaac Toucey of Connecticut, secretary of the navy.

Jacob Thompson of Mississippi, secretary of the interior.

Aaron V. Brown of Tennessee, postmaster-general.

Jeremiah S. Black of Pennsylvania, attorney-general.

Of these men Cobb, Floyd, and Thompson were extreme Secessionists. Many felt that Cobb should have been made President of the Southern Confederacy instead of Davis. In December Thompson went as commissioner from Mississippi to North Carolina to persuade that State to secede, and did not resign his place in the cabinet because, as he said, Mr. Buchanan approved his mission.

Betwixt his own predilections and the influence of these advisers Mr. Buchanan composed for the Thirty-sixth Congress a message which carried consternation among all Unionists. It was of little consequence that he declared the present situation to be the "natural effect" of the "long-continued and intemperate interference" of the Northern people with slavery. But it was of the most serious consequence that, while he condemned secession as unconstitutional, he also declared himself powerless to prevent it. His duty "to take care that the laws be faithfully executed" he knew no other way to perform except by aiding federal officers in the performance of their duties. But where, as in South Carolina, the federal officers had all resigned, so that none remained to be aided, what was he to do? This was practically to take the position that half a dozen men, by resigning their offices, could make the preservation of the Union by its chief executive impossible! Besides this, Mr. Buchanan said that he had "no authority to decide what should be the relations between the Federal government and South Carolina." He afterward said that he desired to avoid a collision of arms "between this and any other government." He did not seem to reflect that he had no right to recognize a State of the Union as being an "other government," in the sense in which he used the phrase, and that, by his very abstention from the measures necessary for maintaining unchanged that relationship which had hitherto existed, he became a party to the establishment of a new relationship, and that, too, of a character which he himself alleged to be unconstitutional. In truth, his chief purpose was to rid himself of any responsibility and to lay it all upon Congress. Yet he was willing to advise Congress as to its powers and duties in the business

It was a misfortune for Abraham Lincoln, which cannot be overrated, that from the moment of his nomination to the day of his death the "Tribune" was largely engaged in criticising his measures and in condemning his policy.

which he shirked in favor of that body, saying that the power to coerce a seceding State had not been delegated to it, and adding the warning that "the Union can never be cemented by the blood of its citizens shed in civil war." So the nation learned that its ruler was of opinion that to resist the destruction of its nationality was both unlawful and inexpedient.

If the conclusions of the message aroused alarm and indignation, its logic excited ridicule. Senator Hale gave a not unfair synopsis: The President, he said, declares: 1. That South Carolina has just cause for seceding. 2. That she has no right to secede. 3. That we have no right to prevent her from seceding; and that the power of the government is "a power to do nothing at all." Another wit said that Buchanan was willing to give up a *part* of the Constitution, and, if necessary, the *whole*, in order to preserve the *remainder*! But while this message of Mr. Buchanan has been bitterly denounced, and with entire justice, from the hour of its transmission to the present day, yet a palliating consideration ought to be noted: he had little reason to believe that, if he asserted the right and duty of forcible coercion, he would find at his back the indispensable force, moral and physical, of the people. Demoralization at the North was widespread. After the lapse of a few months this condition passed, and then those who had been beneath its influence desired to forget the humiliating fact, and hoped that others might either forget or never know the measure of their weakness. In order that they might save their good names, it was natural that they should seek to suppress all evidence which had not already found its way upon the public record; but enough remains to show how grievously for a while the knees were weakened under many who enjoy—and rightfully, by reason of the rest of their lives—the reputation of stalwart patriots. For example, late in October, General Scott suggested to the President a division of the country into four separate confederacies, roughly outlining their boundaries. Scott was a dull man, but he was the head of the army and enjoyed a certain prestige, so that it was impossible to say that his notions, however foolish in themselves, were of no consequence. But if the blunders of General Scott could not fatally wound the Union cause, the blunders of Horace Greeley might conceivably do so. If there had been in the Northern States any newspaper—apart from Mr. Garrison's "Liberator"—which was thoroughly committed to the anti-slavery cause, it was the New York "Tribune," under the guidance of that distinguished editor. Republicans everywhere throughout the land had been educated by his teachings, and had become accustomed to take a large part of their knowledge and their opinions in matters political from his writings. It was a misfortune for Abraham Lincoln, which cannot be overrated, that from the moment of his nomination to the day of his death the "Tribune" was largely engaged in criticising his measures and in condemning his policy.

No sooner did all that, which Mr. Greeley had been striving during many years to bring about, seem to be on the point of consummation, than the demoralized and panic-stricken reformer became desirous to undo his own achievements, and to use for the purpose of effecting a sudden retrogression all the influence which he had gained by bold leadership. November 9, 1860, it was appalling to read in the editorial columns of his sheet, that "if the Cotton States shall decide that they can do better out of the Union than in it, we insist on letting them go in peace;" that, while the "Tribune" denied the right of nullification, yet it would admit that "to withdraw from the Union is quite another matter;" that "whenever a considerable section of our Union shall deliberately resolve to go out, we shall resist all coercive measures designed to keep it in." At the end of another month the "Tribune's" famous editor was still in the same frame of mind, declaring himself "averse to the employment of military force to fasten one section of our confederacy to the other," and saying that, "if eight States, having five millions of people, choose to separate from us, they cannot be permanently withheld from so doing by federal cannon." On December 17 he even said that the South had as good a right to secede from the Union as the colonies had to secede from Great Britain, and that he "would not stand up for coercion, for subjugation," because he did not "think it would be just." On February 23, 1861, he said that if the Cotton States, or the Gulf States, "choose to form an independent nation, they have a clear moral right to do so," and if the "great body of the Southern people" become alienated from the Union and wish to "escape from it, we will do our best to forward their views." A volume could be filled with the like writing of his prolific pen at this time, and every sentence of such purport was the casting of a new stone to create an almost impassable obstruction in the path along which the new President must soon endeavor to move. Thurlow Weed, editor of the Albany "Evening Journal," and the confidential adviser of Seward, wrote in favor of concessions; he declared that "a victorious party can afford to be tolerant;" and he advocated a convention to revise the Constitution, on the ground that, "after more than seventy years of wear and tear, of collision and abrasion, it should be no cause of wonder that the machinery of government is found weakened, or out of repair, or even defective." Frequently he uttered the wish, vague and of fine sound, but enervating, that the Republicans might "meet secession as patriots and not as partisans." On November 9 the Democratic New York "Herald," discussing the election of Lincoln, said: "For far less than this our fathers seceded from Great Britain;" it also declared coercion to be "out of the question," and laid down the principle that each State possesses "the right to break the tie of the confederacy, as a nation might break a treaty, and to repel coercion as a nation might repel invasion."

Local elections in New York and Massachusetts "showed a striking and general reduction of Republican strength." In December the mayor of Philadelphia, though that city had polled a heavy Republican majority, told a mass meeting in Independence Square that denunciations of slavery were inconsistent with national brotherhood, and "must be frowned down by a just and law-abiding people." The Bell and Everett men, generally, desired peace at any price. The business men of the North, alarmed at the prospect of disorder, became loudly solicitous for concession, compromise, even surrender. In Democratic meetings a threatening tone was adopted. One proposal was to reconstruct the Union, leaving out the New England States. So late even as January 21, 1861, before an immense and noteworthy gathering in New York, an orator ventured to say: "If a revolution of force is to begin, it shall be inaugurated at home;" and the words were cheered. The distinguished Chancellor Walworth said that it would be "as brutal to send men to butcher our own brothers of the Southern States as it would be to massacre them in the

Matters looked even worse for the Union cause in Congress than in the country. The prevalent desire was for compromise.

Northern States." When DeWitt Clinton's son, George, spoke of secession as "rebellion," the multitude hailed the word with cries of dissent. Even at Faneuil Hall, in Boston, "a very large and respectable meeting" was emphatically in favor of compromise. It was impossible to measure accurately the extent and force of all this demoralization; but the symptoms were that vast numbers were infected with such sentiments, and that they would have been worse than useless as backers of a vigorous policy on the part of the government.

With the North wavering and ready to retreat, and the South aggressive and confident, it was exacting to expect Mr. Buchanan to stand up for a fight. Why should he, with his old-time Democratic principles, now by a firm, defiant attitude precipitate a crisis, possibly a civil war, when Horace Greeley and Wendell Phillips were conspicuously running away from the consequences of their own teachings, and were loudly crying "Peace! peace!" after they themselves had long been doing all in their power to bring the North up to the fighting point? When these leaders faced to the rear, it was hard to say who could be counted upon to fill the front rank. In truth, it was a situation which might have discouraged a more combative patriot than Buchanan. Meanwhile, while the Northerners talked chiefly of yielding, the hot and florid rhetoric of the Southern orators, often laden with contemptuous insult, smote with disturbing menace upon the ears even of the most courageous Unionists. It was said at the South and feared at the North that secession had a "Spartan band in every Northern State," and that blood would flow in Northern cities at least as soon and as freely as on the Southern plantations, if forcible coercion should be attempted. Was it possible to be sure that this was all rodomontade? To many good citizens there seemed some reason to think that the best hope for avoiding the fulfillment at the North of these sanguinary threats might lie in the probability that the anti-slavery agitators would not stand up to encounter a genuinely mortal peril.

When the Star of the West retired, a little ignominiously, from her task of reinforcing Fort Sumter, Senator Wigfall jeered insolently. "Your flag has been insulted," he said; "redress it if you dare! You have submitted to it for two months, and you will submit forever.... We have dissolved the Union; mend it if you can; cement it with blood; try the experiment!" Mr. Chestnut of South Carolina wished to "unfurl the Palmetto flag, fling it to the breeze ... and ring the clarion notes of defiance in the ears of an insolent foe." Such bombastic but confident language, of which a great quantity was uttered in this winter of 1860-61, may exasperate or intimidate according to the present temper of the opponent whose ear it assaults; for a while the North was more in condition to be awestruck than to be angered. Her spokesmen failed to answer back, and left her to listen not without anxiety to fierce predictions that Southern flags would soon be floating over the dome of the Capitol and even over Faneuil Hall, if she should be so imprudent as to test Southern valor and Southern resources.

Matters looked even worse for the Union cause in Congress than in the country. Occasionally some irritated Northern Republican shot out words of spirit; but the prevalent desire was for conciliation, compromise, and concession, while some actually adopted secession doctrines. For example, Daniel E. Sickles, in the House, threatened that the secession of the Southern States should be followed by that of New York city; and in fact the scheme had been recommended by the Democratic mayor, Fernando Wood, in a message to the Common Council of the city on January 6; and General Dix conceived it to be a possibility. In the Senate Simon Cameron declared himself desirous to preserve the Union "by any sacrifice of feeling, and I may say of principle." A sacrifice of political principle by Cameron was not, perhaps, a serious matter; but he intended the phrase to be emphatic, and he was a leading Republican politician, had been a candidate for the presidential nomination, and was dictator in Pennsylvania. Even Seward, in the better days of the middle of January, felt that he could "afford to meet prejudice with conciliation, exaction with concession which surrenders no principle, and violence with the right hand of peace;" and he was "willing, after the excitement of rebellion and secession should have passed away, to call a convention for amending the Constitution."

This message of Buchanan marked the lowest point to which the temperature of his patriotism fell. Soon afterward, stimulated by heat applied from outside, it began to rise. The first intimation which impressed upon his anxious mind that he was being too acquiescent towards the South came from General Cass. That steadfast Democrat, of the old Jacksonian school, like many of his party at the North, was fully as good a patriot and Union man as most of the Republicans were approving themselves to be during these winter months of vacillation, alarm, and compromise. In November he was strenuously in favor of forcibly coercing a seceding State, but later assented to the tenor of Mr. Buchanan's message. The frame of mind which induced this assent, however, was transitory; for immediately he began to insist upon the reinforcement of the garrisons of the Southern forts, and on December 13 he resigned because the President refused to accede to his views. A few days earlier Howell Cobb had had the grace to resign from the Treasury, which he left entirely empty. In the reorganization Philip F. Thomas of Maryland, a Secessionist also, succeeded Cobb; Judge Black was moved into the State Department; and Edwin M. Stanton of Pennsylvania followed Black as attorney-general. Mr. Floyd, than whom no Secessionist has left a name in worse odor at the North, had at first advised against any "rash movement" in the way of secession, on the ground that Mr. Lincoln's administration would "fail, and be regarded as impotent for good or evil, within four months after his inauguration." None the less he had long been using his official position in the War Department to send arms into the Southern States, and to make all possible arrangements for putting them in an advantageous position for hostilities. Fortunately about this time the famous defalcation in the Indian Department, in which he was guiltily involved, destroyed his credit with the President, and at the same time he quarreled with his associates concerning Anderson's removal to Fort Sumter. On December 29 he resigned, and the duties of his place were laid for a while upon Judge Holt, the postmaster-general.

On Sunday morning, December 30, there was what has been properly called a cabinet crisis. The South Carolina commissioners, just arrived in Washington, were demanding recognition, and to treat with the government as if they were representatives of a foreign power. The President declined to receive them in a diplomatic character, but offered to act as go-between betwixt them and Congress. The President's advisers, however, were in a far less amiable frame of mind, for their blood had been stirred wholesomely by the secession of South Carolina and the presence of these emissaries with their insolent demands. Mr. Black, now at the head of the State Department, had gone through much the same phases of feeling as General Cass. In November he had been "emphatic in his advocacy of coercion," but afterward had approved the President's message and even declared forcible coercion to be "*ipso facto* an expulsion" of the State from the Union; since then he had drifted back and made fast at his earlier moorings. On this important Sunday morning Mr. Buchanan learned with dismay that either his reply to the South Carolinians must be substantially modified, or Mr. Black and Mr. Stanton would retire from the cabinet. Under this pressure he yielded. Mr. Black drafted a new reply to the commissioners, Mr. Stanton copied it, Holt concurred in it, and, in substance, Mr. Buchanan accepted it. This affair constituted, as Messrs. Nicolay and Hay well say, "the President's virtual abdication," and thereafterward began the "cabinet régime." Upon the commissioners this chill gust from the North struck so disagreeably that, on January 2, they hastened home to their "independent nation." From this time forth the South covered Mr. Buchanan with contumely and abuse; Mr. Benjamin called him "a senile executive, under the sinister influence of insane counsels;" and the poor old man, really wishing to do right, but stripped of friends and of his familiar advisers, and confounded by the views of new counselors, presented a spectacle for pity.

On January 8 Mr. Thompson, secretary of the interior, resigned, and the vacancy was left unfilled. A more important change took place on the following day, when Mr. Thomas left the Treasury Department, and the New York bankers, whose aid was essential, forced the President, sorely against his will, to give the place to General John A. Dix. This proved an excellent appointment. General Dix was an old Democrat, but of the high-spirited type; he could have tolerated secession by peaceable agreement, but rose in anger at menaces against the flag and the Union. He conducted his department with entire success, and also rendered to the country perhaps the greatest service that was done by any man during that winter. On January 29 he sent the telegram which closed with

Lincoln's own opinion as to the danger is not quite clear. "I did not then, nor do I now, believe I should have been assassinated, had I gone through Baltimore as first contemplated; but I thought it wise to run no risk, where no risk was necessary."

the famous words: "If any one attempts to haul down the American flag, shoot him on the spot." This rung out as the first cheering, stimulating indication of a fighting temper at the North. It was a tonic which came at a time of sore need, and for too long a while it remained the solitary dose!

So much of the President's message as concerned the condition of the country was referred in the House to a Committee of Thirty-three, composed by appointing one member from each State. Other resolutions and motions upon the same subject, to the number of twenty-five, were also sent to this committee. It had many sessions from December 11 to January 14, but never made an approach to evolving anything distantly approaching agreement.

When, on January 14, the report came, it was an absurd fiasco: it contained six propositions, of which each had the assent of a majority of a quorum; but seven minority reports, bearing together the signatures of fourteen members, were also submitted; and the members of the seceding States refused to act. The only actual fruit was a proposed amendment to the Constitution: "That no amendment shall be made to the Constitution which will authorize or give to Congress the power to abolish or interfere, within any State, with the domestic institutions thereof, including that of persons held to labor or service by the laws of said State." In the expiring hours of the Thirty-sixth Congress this was passed by the House, and then by the Senate, and was signed by the President. Lincoln, in his inaugural address, said of it: "Holding such a provision to be

Many millions of people in the country hated him with a hatred unutterable; among them might well be many fanatics, to whom assassination would seem a noble act.

now constitutional law, I have no objection to its being made express and irrevocable." This view of it was correct; it had no real significance, and the ill-written sentence never disfigured the Constitution; it simply sank out of sight, forgotten by every one.

Collaterally with the sitting of this House committee, a Committee of Thirteen was appointed in the Senate. To these gentlemen also "a string of Union-saving devices" was presented, but on the last day of the year they reported that they had "not been able to agree upon any general plan of adjustment."

The earnest effort of the venerable Crittenden to effect a compromise aroused a faint hope. But he offered little else than an extension westward of the Missouri Compromise line; and he never really had the slightest chance of effecting that consummation, which in fact *could not be* effected. His plan was finally defeated on the last evening of the session.

Collaterally with these congressional debates there were also proceeding in Washington the sessions of the Peace Congress, another futile effort to concoct a cure for an incurable condition. It met on February 4, 1861, but only twenty-one States out of thirty-four were represented. The seven States which had seceded said that they could not come, being "Foreign Nations." Six other States— Arkansas, California, Michigan, Minnesota, Oregon, and Wisconsin—held aloof. Those Northern States which sent delegates selected "their most conservative and compromising men," and so great a tendency towards concession was shown that Unionists soon condemned the scheme as merely a deceitful cover devised by the Southerners behind which they could the more securely carry on their processes of secession. These gentlemen talked a great deal and finally presented a report or plan to Congress five days before the end of the session; the House refused to receive it, the Senate rejected it by 7 ayes to 28 nays. The only usefulness of the gathering was as evidence of the unwillingness of the South to compromise. In fact the Southern leaders were entirely frank and outspoken in acknowledging their position; they had said, from the beginning, that they did not wish the Committee of Thirty-three to accomplish anything; and they had endeavored to dissuade Southerners from accepting positions upon it. Hawkins of Florida said that "the time of compromise had passed forever." South Carolina refused to share in the Peace Congress, because she did "not deem it advisable to initiate negotiations when she had no desire or intention to promote the object in view." Governor Peters of Mississippi, in poetic language, suggested another difficulty: "When sparks cease to fly upwards," he said, "Comanches respect treaties, and wolves kill sheep no more, the oath of a Black Republican might be of some value as a protection to slave property." Jefferson Davis contemptuously stigmatized all the schemes of compromise as "quack nostrums," and he sneered justly enough at those who spun fine arguments of legal texture, and consumed time "discussing abstract questions, reading patchwork from the opinions of men now mingled with the dust."

It is not known by what logic gentlemen who held these views defended their conduct in retaining their positions in the government of the nation for the purpose of destroying it. Senator Yulee of Florida shamelessly gave his motive for staying in the Senate: "It is thought we can keep the hands of Mr.

Buchanan tied and disable the Republicans from effecting any legislation which will strengthen the hands of the incoming administration." Mr. Toombs of Georgia, speaking and voting at his desk in the Senate, declared himself "as good a rebel and as good a traitor as ever descended from Revolutionary loins," and said that the Union was already dissolved,—by which assertion he made his position in the Senate absolutely indefensible. The South Carolina senators resigned before their State ordained itself a "foreign nation," and incurred censure for being so "precipitate." In a word, the general desire was to remain in office, hampering and obstructing the government, until March 4, 1861, and at a caucus of disunionists it was agreed to do so. But the pace became too rapid, and resignations followed pretty close upon the formal acts of secession.

On the same day on which the Peace Congress opened its sessions in Washington, there came together at Montgomery, in Alabama, delegates from six States for the purpose of forming a Southern Confederacy. On the third day thereafter a plan for a provisional government, substantially identical with the Constitution of the United States, was adopted. On February 9 the oath of allegiance was taken, and Jefferson Davis and Alexander H. Stephens were elected respectively President and Vice-President. On February 13 the military and naval committees were directed to report plans for organizing an army and navy. Mr. Davis promptly journeyed to Montgomery, making on the way many speeches, in which he told his hearers that no plan for a reconstruction of the old Union would be entertained; and promised that those who should interfere with the new nation would have to "smell Southern powder and to feel Southern steel." On February 18 he was inaugurated, and in his address again referred to the "arbitrament of the sword." Immediately afterward he announced his cabinet as follows:—

Robert Toombs of Georgia, secretary of state.
C.G. Memminger of South Carolina, secretary of the treasury.
L.P. Walker of Alabama, secretary of war.
S.R. Mallory of Florida, secretary of the navy.
J.H. Reagan of Texas, postmaster-general.
Judah P. Benjamin of Louisiana, attorney-general.

On March 11 the permanent Constitution was adopted. Thus the machine of the new government was set in working order. Mr. Greeley gives some interesting figures showing the comparative numerical strength of the sections of the country at this time:—

The free population of the seven States which had seceded, was 2,656,948
The free population of the eight slave States which had not seceded, was 5,633,005
Total 8,289,953
The slaves in the States of the first list were .2,312,046
The slaves in the States of the second list were 1,638,297
Total of slaves 3,950,343
The population of the whole Union by the census of 1860, was 31,443,321

The disproportion would have discouraged the fathers of the new nation, if they had anticipated that the North would be resolute in using its overwhelming resources. But how could they believe that this would be the case when they read the New York "Tribune" and the reports of Mr. Phillips's harangues?

On February 13 the electoral vote was to be counted in Congress. Rumors were abroad that the Secessionists intended to interfere with this by tumults and violence; but the evidence is insufficient to prove that any such scheme was definitely matured; it was talked of, but ultimately it seems to have been laid aside with a view to action at a later date. Naturally enough, however, the country was disquieted. In the emergency the action of General Scott was watched with deep anxiety. A Southerner by birth and by social sympathies, he had been expected by the Secessionists to join their movement. But the old soldier—though broken by age and infirmities, and though he had proposed the folly of voluntarily quartering the country, like the corpse of a traitor—had his patriotism and his temper at once aroused when violence was threatened. On and after October 29 he had repeatedly advised reinforcement of the Southern garrisons; though it must be admitted, in Buchanan's behalf, that the general made no suggestion as to how or where the troops could be obtained for this purpose. In the same spirit he now said, with stern resolution, that there should be ample military preparations to insure both the count and the inauguration;

and he told some of the Southerners that he would blow traitors to pieces at the cannon's mouth without hesitation. Disturbed at his vehemence, they denounced him bitterly, and sent him frequent notices of assassination. Floyd distributed orders concerning troops and munitions directly from the War Department, and carefully concealed them from the general who was the head of the army. But secrecy and intimidation were in vain. The aged warrior was fiercely in earnest; if there was going to be any outbreak in Washington he was going to put it down with bullets and bayonets, and he gathered his soldiers and instructed his officers accordingly. But happily the preparation of these things was sufficient to render the use of them unnecessary. When the day came Vice-President Breckenridge performed his duty, however unwelcome, without flinching. He presided over the joint session and conducted the count with the air of a man determined to enforce law and order, and at the close declared the election of Abraham Lincoln and Hannibal Hamlin.

The custom of the country compelled this man, whom it had long since selected as its ruler, to make a journey of extreme danger without any species of protection whatsoever.

Still only the smaller crisis had been passed. Much more alarming stories now flew from mouth to mouth,—of plots to seize the capital and to prevent the inauguration, even to assassinate Lincoln on his journey to Washington. How much foundation there was for these is not accurately known. That the idea of capturing Washington had fascinated the Southern fancy is certain. "I see no reason," said Senator Iverson, "why Washington city should not be continued the capital of the Southern Confederacy." The Richmond "Examiner" railed grossly: "That filthy cage of unclean birds must and will assuredly be purified by fire…. Our people can take it,—they will take it…. Scott, the arch-traitor, and Lincoln, the beast, combined, cannot prevent it. The 'Illinois Ape' must retrace his journey more rapidly than he came." The abundant talk of this sort created uneasiness; and Judge Holt said that there was cause for alarm. But a committee of Congress reported that, though it was difficult to speak positively, yet they found no evidence sufficient to prove "the existence of a secret organization." Alexander H. Stephens has denied that there was any intention to attack the city, and probably the notion of seizure did not pass beyond the stage of talk.

But the alleged plot to assassinate Mr. Lincoln was more definite. He had been spending the winter quietly in Springfield, where he had been overrun by visitors, who wished to look at him, to advise him, and to secure promises of office; fortunately the tedious procession had lost part of its offensiveness by touching his sense of humor. Anxious people made well-meaning but useless efforts to induce him to say something for effect upon the popular mind; but he resolutely and wisely maintained silence. His position and opinions, he said, had already been declared in his speeches with all the clearness he could give to them, and the people had appeared to understand and approve them. He could not improve and did not desire to change these utterances. Occasionally he privately expressed his dislike to the conceding and compromising temper which threatened to undo, for an indefinite future, all which the long and weary struggle of anti-slavery men had accomplished. In this line he wrote a letter of protest to Greeley, which inspired that gentleman to a singular expression of sympathy; let the Union go to pieces, exclaimed the emotional editor, let presidents be assassinated, let the Republican party suffer crushing defeat, but let there not be "another nasty compromise." To Mr. Kellogg, the Illinoisian on the House Committee of Thirty-three, Lincoln wrote: "Entertain no proposition for a compromise in regard to the extension of slavery. The instant you do, they have us under again; all our labor is lost, and sooner or later must be done over again." He repeated almost the same words to E. B. Washburne, a member of the House. Duff Green tried hard to get something out of him for the comfort of Mr. Buchanan, but failed to extort more than commonplace generalities. To Seward he wrote that he did not wish to interfere with the present status, or to meddle with slavery as it now lawfully existed. To like purport he wrote to Alexander H. Stephens, induced thereto by the famous Union speech of that gentleman. He eschewed hostile feeling, saying: "I never have been, am not now, and probably never shall be, in a mood of harassing the people, either North or South." Nevertheless, while he said that all were "brothers of a common country," he was perfectly resolved that the country should remain "common," even if the bond of brotherhood had to be riveted by force. He admitted that this necessity would be "an ugly point;" but he was perfectly clear that "the right of a State to secede is not an open or debatable question." He desired that General Scott should be prepared either to "hold or retake" the Southern forts, if need should be, at or after the inauguration; but on his journey to Washington he said to many audiences that he wished no war and no bloodshed, and that these evils could be avoided if people would only "keep cool" and "keep their temper, on both sides of the line."

On Monday, February 11, 1861, Mr. Lincoln spoke to his fellow citizens of Springfield a very brief farewell, so solemn as to sound ominous in the ears of those who know what afterward occurred. It was arranged that he should stop at various points upon the somewhat circuitous route which had been laid out, and that he should arrive in Washington on Saturday, February 23. The programme was pursued accurately till near the close; he made, of course, many speeches, but none added anything to what was already known as to his views.

Meantime the thick rumors of violence were bringing much uneasiness to persons who were under responsibilities. Baltimore was the place where, and its villainous "Plug Uglies" were the persons by whom, the plot, if there was one, was to be executed. Mr. Felton, president of the Philadelphia, Wilmington and Baltimore Railroad Company, engaged Allan Pinkerton to explore the matter, and the report of this skillful detective indicated a probability of an attack with the purpose of assassination. At that time the cars were drawn by horses across town from the northern to the southern station, and during the passage an assault could be made with ease and with great chance of success. As yet there was no indication that the authorities intended to make, even if they could make, any adequate arrangements for the protection of the traveler. At Philadelphia Mr. Lincoln was told of the fears of his friends, and talked with Mr. Pinkerton, but he refused to change his plan. On February 22 he was to assist at a flag-raising in Philadelphia, and was then to go on to Harrisburg, and on the following day he was to go from there to Baltimore. He declined to alter either route or hours.

But other persons besides Mr. Felton had been busy with independent detective investigations, the result of which was in full accord with the report of Mr. Pinkerton. On February 22 Mr. Frederick W. Seward, sent by his father and General Scott, both then at Washington, delivered to Mr. Lincoln, at Philadelphia, the message that there was "serious danger" to his life if the time of his passage through Baltimore should be known. Yet Lincoln still remained obdurate. He declared that if an escorting delegation from Baltimore should meet him at Harrisburg, he would go on with it. But at Harrisburg no such escort presented itself. Then the few who knew the situation discussed further as to what should be done, Norman B. Judd being chief spokesman for evading the danger by a change of programme. Naturally the objection of seeming timid and of exciting ridicule was present in the minds of all, and it was put somewhat emphatically by Colonel Sumner. Mr. Lincoln at last settled the dispute; he said:

Ungainly they saw him, but not undignified, and the strange impressive sadness seldom dwelt so strikingly upon his face as at this time, as though all the weight of misery, which the millions of his fellow citizens were to endure throughout the coming years, already burdened [his] soul.

"I have thought over this matter considerably since I went over the ground with Pinkerton last night. The appearance of Mr. Frederick Seward, with warning from another source, confirms Mr. Pinkerton's belief. Unless there are some other reasons besides fear of ridicule, I am disposed to carry out Judd's plan."

This plan was accordingly carried out with the success which its simplicity insured. Mr. Lincoln and his stalwart friend, Colonel Lamon, slipped out of a side door to a hackney carriage, were driven to the railway station, and returned by the train to Philadelphia. Their departure was not noticed, but had it been, news of it could not have been sent away, for Mr. Felton had had the telegraph wires secretly cut outside the town. He also ordered, upon a plausible pretext, that the southward-bound night train on his road should be held back until the arrival of this train from Harrisburg. Mr. Lincoln and Colonel Lamon passed from the one train to the other without recognition, and rolled into Washington early on the following morning. Mr. Seward and Mr. Washburne met Lincoln at the station and went with him to Willard's Hotel. Soon afterward the country was astonished, and perhaps some persons were discomfited, as the telegraph carried abroad the news of his arrival.

Those who were disappointed at this safe conclusion of his journey, if in fact there were any such, together with many who would have contemned assassination, at once showered upon him sneers and ridicule. They said that Lincoln had put on a disguise and had shown the white feather, when there had been no real danger. But this was not just. Whether or not there was the completed machinery of a definite, organized plot for assault and assassination is uncertain; that is to say, this is not *proved*; yet the evidence is so strong that the majority of investigators seem to agree in the opinion that *probably* there was a plan thoroughly concerted and ready for execution. Even if there was not, it was very likely that a riot might be suddenly started, which would be as fatal in its consequences as a premeditated scheme. But, after all, the question of the plot is one of mere curiosity and quite aside from the true issue. That issue, so far as it presented itself for determination by Mr. Lincoln, was simply whether a case of such probability of danger was made out that as a prudent man he should overrule the only real objection,—that of exciting ridicule,—and avoid a peril which the best judges believed to exist, and which, if it did exist, involved consequences of immeasurable seriousness not only to himself but to the nation. For a wise man only one conclusion was possible. The story of the disguise was a silly slander, based upon the trifling fact that for this night journey Lincoln wore a traveling cap instead of his hat.

Lincoln's own opinion as to the danger is not quite clear. He said to Mr. Lossing that, after hearing Mr. Seward, he believed "such a plot to be in existence." But he also said: "I did not then, nor do I now, believe I should have been assassinated, had I gone through Baltimore as first contemplated; but I thought it wise to run no risk, where no risk was necessary."

The reflection can hardly fail to occur, how grossly unfair it was that Mr. Lincoln should be put into the position in which he was put at this time, and then that fault should be found with him even if his prudence was overstrained. Many millions of people in the country hated him with a hatred unutterable; among them might well be many fanatics, to whom assassination would seem a noble act, many desperadoes who would regard it as a pleasing excitement; and he was to go through a city which men of this stamp could at any time dominate. The custom of the country compelled this man, whom it had long since selected as its ruler, to make a journey of extreme danger without any species of protection whatsoever. So far as peril went, no other individual in the United States had ever, presumably, been in a peril like that which beset him; so far as safeguards went, he had no more than any other traveler. A few friends volunteered to make the journey with him, but they were useless as guardians; and he and they were so hustled and jammed in the railway stations that one of them actually had his arm broken. This extraordinary spectacle may have indicated folly on the part of the nation which permitted it, but certainly it did not involve the disgrace of the individual who had no choice about it. The people put Mr. Lincoln in a position in which he was subjected to the most appalling, as it is the most vague, of all dangers, and then left him to take care of himself as best he could. It was ungenerous afterward to criticise him for exercising prudence in the performance of that duty which he ought never to have been called upon to perform at all.

Immediately after his arrival in Washington Mr. Lincoln received a visit from the members of the Peace Congress. Grotesque and ridiculous descriptions of him, as if he had been a Caliban in education, manners, and aspect, had been rife among Southerners, and the story goes that the Southern delegates expected to be at once amused and shocked by the sight of a clodhopper whose conversation would be redolent of the barnyard, not to say of the pigsty. Those of them who had any skill in reading character were surprised,— as the tradition is,—discomfited, even a little alarmed, at what in fact they beheld; for Mr. Lincoln appeared before them a self-possessed man, expressing to them such clear convictions and such a distinct and firm purpose as compelled them into new notions of his capacity and told them of much trouble ahead. His remark to Mr. Rives, coming from one who spoke accurately, had an ominous sound in rebellious ears: "My course is as plain as a turnpike road. It is marked out by the Constitution. I am in no doubt which way to go." The wiser Southerners withdrew from this reception quite sober and thoughtful, with some new ideas about the man with whom their relationship seemed on the verge of becoming hostile. After abundant allowance is made for the enthusiasm of Northern admirers, it remains certain that Lincoln bore well this severe ordeal of criticism on the part of those who would have been glad to despise him. Ungainly they saw him, but not undignified, and the strange impressive sadness seldom dwelt so strikingly upon his face as at this time, as though all the weight of misery, which the millions of his fellow citizens were to endure throughout the coming years, already burdened the soul of the ruler who had been chosen to play the most responsible part in the crisis and the anguish.

March 4, 1861, inauguration day, was fine and sunny. If there had ever been any real danger of trouble, the fear of it had almost entirely subsided. Northerners and Southerners had found out in good season that General Scott was not in a temporizing mood; he had in the city two batteries, a few companies of regulars,—653 men, exclusive of some marines,—and the corps of picked Washington Volunteers. He said that this force was all he wanted.

The inaugural address was simple, earnest, and direct, unincumbered by that rhetorical ornamentation which the American people have always admired as the highest form of eloquence.

President Buchanan left the White House in an open carriage, escorted by a company of sappers and miners under Captain Duane. At Willard's Hotel Mr. Lincoln entered the carriage, and the two gentlemen passed along the avenue, through crowds which cheered but made no disturbance, to the Capitol. General

Scott with his regulars marched, "flanking the movement, in parallel streets." His two batteries, while not made unpleasantly conspicuous, yet controlled the plateau which extends before the east front of the Capitol. Mr. Lincoln was simply introduced by Senator Baker of Oregon, and delivered his inaugural address. His voice had great carrying capacity, and the vast crowd heard with ease a speech of which every sentence was fraught with an importance and scrutinized with an anxiety far beyond that of any other speech ever delivered in the United States. At its close the venerable Chief Justice Taney administered the oath of office, thereby informally but effectually reversing the most famous opinion delivered by him during his long incumbency in his high office.

The inaugural address was simple, earnest, and direct, unincumbered by that rhetorical ornamentation which the American people have always admired as the highest form of eloquence. Those Northerners who had expected magniloquent periods and exaggerated outbursts of patriotism were disappointed; and as they listened in vain for the scream of the eagle, many grumbled at the absence of what they conceived to be *force*. Yet the general feeling was of satisfaction, which grew as the address was more thoroughly studied. The Southerners, upon their part, looking anxiously to see whether or not they must fight for their purpose, construed the words of the new President correctly. They heard him say: "The union of these States is perpetual." "No State upon its own mere motion can lawfully get out of the Union." "I shall take care, as the Constitution itself expressly enjoins upon me, that the laws of the Union be faithfully executed in all the States." He also declared his purpose "to hold, occupy, and possess the property and places belonging to the government, and to collect the duties and imposts." These sentences made up the issue directly with secession, and the South, reading them, knew that, if the North was ready to back the President, war was inevitable; none the less so because Mr. Lincoln closed with patriotic and generous words: "We are not enemies, but friends. We must not be enemies. Though passion may have strained, it must not break our bonds of affection."

Until after the election of Mr. Lincoln in November, 1860, the sole issue between the North and the South, between Republicans on the one hand and

Democrats and Compromisers on the other, had related to slavery. Logically, the position of the Republicans was impregnable. Their platforms and their leaders agreed that the party intended strictly to respect the Constitution, and not to interfere at all with slavery in the States within which it now lawfully existed. They said with truth that they had in no case deprived the slaveholding communities of their rights, and they denied the truth of the charge that they cherished an inchoate design to interfere with those rights; adding very truly that, at worst, a mere design, which did not find expression in an overt act, could give no right of action to the South. Mr. Lincoln had been most explicit in declaring that the opposition to slavery was not to go beyond efforts to prevent its *extension*, which efforts would be wholly within the Constitution and the law. He repeated these things in his inaugural.

But while these incontrovertible allegations gave the Republicans a logical advantage of which they properly made the most, the South claimed a right to make other collateral and equally undeniable facts the ground of action. The only public matter in connection with which Mr. Lincoln had won any reputation was that of slavery. No one could deny that he had been elected because the Republican party had been pleased with his expression of opinion on this subject. Now his most pointed and frequently reiterated expression of that opinion was that slavery was a "moral, social, and political evil;" and this language was a fair equivalent of the statement of the Republican platform of 1856, classing Slavery and Mormonism together, as "twin relics of barbarism." That the North was willing, or would long be willing, to remain in amicable social and political bonds with a moral, social, and political evil, and a relic of barbarism, was intrinsically improbable, and was made more improbable by the symptoms of the times. Indeed, Mr. Seward had said, in famous words, that his section would not play this unworthy part; he had proclaimed already the existence of an "irrepressible conflict;" and therefore the South had the word of the Republican leader that, in spite of the Republican respect for the law, an anti-slavery crusade was already in existence. The Southern chiefs distinctly recognized and accepted this situation. There was an avowed Northern condemnation of their institution; there was an acknowledged "conflict." Such being the case, it was the opinion of the chief men at the South that the position taken by the North, of strict performance of clear

constitutional duties concerning an odious institution, would not suffice for the
safe perpetuation of that institution. This, their judgment, appeared to be in a
certain way also the judgment of Mr. Lincoln; for he also conceived that to put
slavery where the "fathers" had left it was to put it "in the way of ultimate
extinction;" and he had, in the most famous utterance of his life, given his
forecast of the future to the effect that the country would in time be "all free."
The only logical deduction was that he, and the Republican party which had
agreed with him sufficiently to make him president, believed that the South had
no lawful recourse by which this result, however unwelcome or ruinous, could in

> *What was more natural than that he should at
> this moment revert to this great topic and make
> the old dispute the main part and real substance
> of his address? But this fatal error he avoided.*

the long run and the fullness of time be escaped. Under such circumstances
Southern political leaders now decided that the time for separation had come. In
speaking of their scheme they called it "secession," and said that secession was a
lawful act because the Constitution was a compact revocable by any of the
parties. They might have called it "revolution," and have defended it upon the
general right of any large body of people, dissatisfied with the government under
which they find themselves, to cast it off. But, if the step was *revolution*, then the
burden of proof was upon them; whereas they said that *secession* was their lawful
right, without any regard whatsoever to the motive which induced them to
exercise it. Such was the character of the issue between the North and the South
prior to the first ordinance of secession. The action of South Carolina, followed
by the other Gulf States, at once changed that issue, shifting it from pro-slavery
versus anti-slavery to union versus disunion. This alteration quickly compelled
great numbers of men, both at the North and at the South, to reconsider and,
upon a new issue, to place themselves also anew.

It has been said by all writers that in the seven seceding States there was, in the four months following the election, a very large proportion of "Union men." The name only signified that these men did not think that the present inducements to disunion were sufficient to render it a wise measure. It did not signify that they thought disunion unlawful, unconstitutional, and treasonable. When, however, state conventions decided the question of advisability against their opinions, and they had to choose between allegiance to the State and allegiance to the Union, they immediately adhered to the State, and this none the less because they feared that she had taken an ill-advised step. That is to say, at the South a "Union man" *wished* to preserve the Union, whereas at the North a "Union man" recognized a supreme *obligation* to do so.

With unerring judgment he dwelt little on that momentous issue which had only just been displaced, and took his stand fairly upon that still more momentous one which had so newly come up. He spoke for the Union.

While the South, by political alchemy, was becoming solidified and homogeneous, a corresponding change was going on at the North. In that section the great numbers—of whom some would have re-made the Constitution, others would have agreed to peaceable separation, and still others would have made any concession to retain the integrity of the Union—now saw that these were indeed, as Jefferson Davis had said, "quack nostrums," and that the choice lay between permitting a secession accompanied with insulting menaces and some degree of actual violence, and maintaining the Union by coercion. In this dilemma great multitudes of Northern Democrats, whose consciences had never been in the least disturbed by the existence of slavery in the country or even by efforts to extend it, became "Union men" in the Northern sense of the word, which made it about equivalent to coercionists. Their simple creed was the integrity and perpetuity of the nation.

Mr. Lincoln showed in his inaugural his accurate appreciation of the new situation. Owing all that he had become in the world to a few anti-slavery speeches, elevated to the presidency by votes which really meant little else than hostility to slavery, what was more natural than that he should at this moment revert to this great topic and make the old dispute the main part and real substance of his address? But this fatal error he avoided. With unerring judgment he dwelt little on that momentous issue which had only just been displaced, and took his stand fairly upon that still more momentous one which had so newly come up. He spoke for the Union; upon that basis a united North *ought* to support him; upon that basis the more northern of the slave States might remain loyal. As matter of fact, Union had suddenly become the real issue, but it needed at the hands of the President to be publicly and explicitly announced as such; this recognition was essential; he gave it on this earliest opportunity, and the announcement was the first great service of the new Republican ruler. It seems now as though he could hardly have done otherwise, or have fallen into the error of allying himself with bygone or false issues. It may be admitted that he could not have passed this new one by; but the important matter was that of proportion and relation, and in this it was easy to blunder. In truth it was a crisis when blundering was so easy that nearly all the really able men of the North had been doing it badly for three or four months past, and not a few of them were going to continue it for two or three months to come. Therefore the sound conception of the inaugural deserves to be considered as an indication, one among many, of Lincoln's capacity for seeing with entire distinctness the great main fact, and for recognizing it as such. Other matters, which lay over and around such a fact, side issues, questions of detail, affairs of disguise or deception, never confused or misled him. He knew with unerring accuracy where the biggest fact lay, and he always anchored fast to it and stayed with it. For many years he had been anchored to anti-slavery; now, in the face of the nation, he shifted his anchorage to the Union; and each time he held securely.

APPENDIX I

LINCOLN IN HIS OWN HAND

'A HOUSE DIVIDED'

"I do not expect the Union to be dissolved;
I do not expect the house to fall; but I do
expect it will cease to be divided."

Lincoln's letter of February 14, 1860, responding to three Illinois farmers who requested that Lincoln clarify his declaration that "a house divided against itself can not stand."

A transcription of the letter follows.

Springfield, Feb. 14. 1860

Messrs. O. P. Hall
        J. R. Fullinwider
      & W. F. Correll.
              Gentlemen.

                    Your letter, in which, among
other things, you ask "what I meant when
I said this Union could not stand half slave
and half free— and also what I meant
when I said a house divided against itself
could not stand" is received, and I very
cheerfully answer it, as plainly as I may be
able— You misquote, to some material extent, what I did say; which induces me
to think you have not, very carefully, read
the speech in which the expressions occur which
to puzzle you to understand— For this reason, and
because the language I used is as plain as I can
make it,. I now quote at length the whole passage
in which the expressions which puzzle you occur— It
is as follows: "We are now. far into the fifth

year since a policy was initiated with the
avowed object, and confident promise of
putting an end to slavery agitation— Under the
operation of that policy that agitation has
not only not ceased, but constantly augmented.
I believe it will not cease until a crisis
shall have been reached, and passed— A
house divided against itself can not stand—
I believe this government can not endure
permanently, half slave, and half free— I
do not expect the Union to be dissolved;
I do not expect the house to fall; but
I do expect it will cease to be divided—
It will become all one thing, or all the other.
Either the opponents of slavery will arrest the
further spread of it, and place it where the
public mind shall rest in the belief that it is
in course of ultimate extinction; or its advocates will push it forward till it will become
alike lawful in all the states, old as well
as new, North, as well as South".
    That is the whole paragraph; and it puzzles
me to make my meaning plainer— Look over

159

it carefully, and conclude I meant all I said, and
did not mean anything I did not say, and you
will have my meaning— Douglas attacked me
upon this, as saying it was a declaration of war
between the slave and the free states— You will
~~perceive I said no such thing; and I never yet~~
I thought of no such thing—

If I had said "I believe this government can
not _last always_, half slave and half free"
would you understand it any better than
you do?. "Endure permanently" and "last
always" have exactly the same meaning—

If you, or any of you, will state to me
some meaning, which you suppose I had, I
can, and will instantly tell you whether
~~that was my meaning—~~

　　　　　　　　　　Yours very truly
　　　　　　　　　　A. Lincoln

Springfield, Feb. 14. 1860

Messrs. O.P. Hall
  J.R. Fullinwider
  W.F. Correll.
   Gentlemen.

Your letter, in which, among other things, you ask "what I meant when I said this Union could not stand half slave and half free—and also what I meant when I said a house divided against itself could not stand" is received, and I very cheerfully answer it as plainly as I may be able. You misquote, to some material extent, what I did say; which induces me to think you have not, very carefully, read the speech in which the expressions occur which to puzzle you to understand. For this reason, and because the language I used is as plain as I can make it, I now quote at length the whole paragraph in which the expressions which puzzle you occur. It is as follows: "We are now far into the fifth year since a policy was initiated with the avowed object, and confident promise of putting an end to slavery agitation. Under the operation of that policy that agitation has not only not ceased, but constantly augmented. I believe it will not cease until a crisis shall have been reached, and passed. A house divided against itself can not stand. I believe this government can not endure <u>permanently</u>, half slave, and half free. I do not expect the Union to be dissolved; I do not expect the house to fall; but I do expect it will cease to be divided. It will become all one thing, or all the other. Either the opponents of slavery will arrest the further spread of it, and place it where the public mind shall rest in the belief that it is in course of ultimate extinction; or it's advocates will push it forward till it will become alike lawful in all the states, old as well as new, North, as well as South."

That is the whole paragraph; and it puzzles me to make my meaning plainer. Look over it carefully, and conclude I meant all I said, and did not mean anything I did not say, and you will have my meaning. Douglas attacked me upon this, saying it was a declaration of war between the slave and the free states. You will perceive I said no such thing; and I assure you I thought of no such thing.

If I had said "I believe this government can not <u>last always</u>, half slave and half free" would you understand it any better than you do? "Endure permanently" and "last always" have exactly the same meaning.

If you, or any of you, will state to me some meaning which you suppose I had, I can, and will instantly tell you whether that was my meaning.

Yours very truly
  A. Lincoln

APPENDIX II

LINCOLN IN HIS OWN WORDS

INAUGURAL ADDRESS OF 1861

"Continue to execute all the express
provisions of our national
Constitution, and the Union will
endure forever."

The final draft of Lincoln's first inaugural address, delivered March 4, 1861, with Lincoln's handwritten emendations.

A transcription of the inaugural address follows. Page numbers in the margin indicate where each new page of the draft begins.

Note to the Reader: Certain pages of the inaugural address draft are reproduced more than once, to illustrate those sections where Lincoln overlaid a portion of the printed text with his handwritten revisions. This occurs on pages A1, A4, A6, and A7. This page key appears in the upper corner of each facsimile and is not part of the original document.

(March 4, 1861)

I

In compliance with a custom as old as the government itself, I appear before you to address you briefly, and to take, in your presence, the oath prescribed by the Constitution of the United States, to be taken by the President "before he enters on the execution of his office."

The more modern custom of electing a Chief Magistrate upon a previously declared platform of principles, supercedes, in a great measure, the necessity of re-stating those principles in an address of this sort. Upon the plainest grounds of good faith, one so elected is not at liberty to shift his position. It is necessarily implied, if not expressed, that, in his judgment, the platform which he thus accepts, binds him to nothing either unconstitutional or inexpedient.

Having been so elected upon the Chicago Platform, and while I would repeat nothing in it, of aspersion or epithet or question of motive against any man or party, I hold myself bound by duty, as well as impelled by inclination to follow, within the executive sphere, the principles therein declared. By no other course could I meet the reasonable expectations of the country.

I do not consider it necessary at present for me to say more than I have, in relation to those matters of administration, about which there is no special excitement.

Apprehension seems to exist among the people of the Southern States, that by the accession of a Republican Administration, their property, and their peace, and personal security, are to be endangered. There has never been any reasonable cause for such apprehension. Indeed, the most ample evidence to the contrary has all the while existed, and been open to their inspection. It is found in nearly all the published speeches of him who now addresses you. I do but quote from one of those speeches when I declare that "I have no purpose, directly or indirectly, to interfere with the institution of slavery in the States where it exists. I believe I have no lawful right to do so, and I have no inclination to do so." Those who nominated and elected me did so with full knowledge that I had made this, and many similar declarations, and had never recanted them. And more than this, they placed in the platform, for my acceptance, and as a law to themselves, and to me, the clear and emphatic resolution which I now read :

"*Resolved*, That the maintenance inviolate of the rights of the States, and especially the right of each State to order and control its own domestic institutions according to its own judgment exclusively, is essential to that balance of power on which the perfection and endurance of our political fabric depend ; and we denounce the lawless invasion by armed force of the soil of any State or Territory, no matter under what pretext, as among the gravest of crimes."

1

In compliance with a custom as old as the government itself, I appear before you to address you briefly, and to take, in your presence, the oath prescribed by the Constitution of the United States, to be taken by the President "before he enters on the execution of his office."

I do not consider it necessary, at present, for me to discuss those matters of administration about which there is no special anxiety, or excitement.

Apprehension seems to exist among the people of the Southern States, that by the accession of a Republican Administration, their property, and their peace, and personal security, are to be endangered. There has never been any reasonable cause for such apprehension. Indeed, the most ample evidence to the contrary has all the while existed, and been open to their inspection. It is found in nearly all the published speeches of him who now addresses you. I do but quote from one of those speeches when I declare that "I have no purpose, directly or indirectly, to interfere with the institution of slavery in the States where it exists. I believe I have no lawful right to do so, and I have no inclination to do so." Those who nominated and elected me did so with full knowledge that I had made this, and many similar declarations, and had never recanted them. And more than this, they placed in the platform, for my acceptance, and as a law to themselves, and to me, the clear and emphatic resolution which I now read :

"*Resolved,* That the maintenance inviolate of the rights of the States, and especially the right of each State to order and control its own domestic institutions according to its own judgment exclusively, is essential to that balance of power on which the perfection and endurance of our political fabric depend ; and we denounce the lawless invasion by armed force of the soil of any State or Territory, no matter under what pretext, as among the gravest of crimes."

2

I now reiterate these sentiments: and in doing so, I only press upon the public attention the most conclusive evidence of which the case is susceptible, that the property, peace and security of no section are to be in anywise endangered by the now incoming Administration. I add too, that all the protection which, consistently with the Constitution and the laws, can be given, will be cheerfully given to all the States—as cheerfully to one section as to another.

☞ There is much controversy about the delivering up of fugitives from service or labor. The clause I now read is as plainly written in the Constitution as any other of its provisions :

"No person held to service or labor in one State, under the laws thereof, escaping into another, shall, in consequence of any law or regulation therein, be discharged from such service or labor, but shall be delivered up on claim of the party to whom such service or labor may be due."

It is scarcely questioned that this provision was intended by those who made it, for the reclaiming of what we call fugitive slaves; and the intention of the law-giver is the law. All members of Congress swear their support to the whole Constitution—to this provision as much as to any other. To the proposition, then, that slaves whose cases come within the terms of this clause, "shall be delivered up," their oaths are unanimous. Now, if they would make the effort in good temper, could they not, with nearly equal unanimity, frame and pass a law, by means of which to keep good that unanimous oath ?

There is some difference of opinion whether this clause should be enforced by national or by state authority; but surely that difference is not a very material one. If the slave is to be surrendered, it can be of but little consequence to him, or to others, by which authority it is done. And should any one, in any case, be content that his oath shall go unkept, on a merely unsubstantial controversy as to *how* it shall be kept ?

Again, in any law upon this subject, ought not all the safeguards of liberty known in civilized and humane jurisprudence to be introduced, so that a free man be not, in any case, surrendered as a slave ? *And might it not be well*

☞ I take the official oath to-day, with no mental reservations, and with no purpose to construe the Constitution or laws, by any hypercritical rules. And while I do not ~~choose~~ now to specify particular acts of Congress as proper to be enforced, I do suggest, that it will be much safer for all, both in official and private stations, to conform to, and abide by, all those acts which stand unrepealed, than to violate any of them, trusting to find impunity in having them held to be unconstitutional.

when lawfully demanded, for whatever cause—

at the same time, to provide by law for the enforcement of that clause in the Constitution which guaranties that "The citizens of each State shall be entitled to all privileges and immunities of citizens in the several States"?

3

It is ~~now~~ seventy-two years since the first inauguration of a President under our national Constitution. During that period fifteen different and greatly distinguished citizens, have, in succession, administered the executive branch of the government. They have conducted it through many perils; and, *generally,* with great success. Yet, with all this scope for precedent, I now enter upon the same task for the brief constitutional term of four years, under great and peculiar difficulty. A disruption of the Federal Union *heretofore only menaced, is now formidably attempted.* ~~heretofore only menaced. The particulars of what has been done so generally and freely, that I need not to waste any time in recounting them.~~

I hold, that in contemplation of universal law, and of the Constitution, the Union of these States is perpetual. Perpetuity is implied, if not expressed, in the fundamental law of all national governments. It is safe to assert that no government proper, ever had a provision in its organic law for its own termination. Continue to execute all the express provisions of our national Constitution, and the Union will endure forever—it being impossible to destroy it, except by some action not provided for in the instrument itself.

Again, if the United States be not a government proper, but an association of States in the nature of contract merely, can it, as a contract, be peaceably unmade, by less than all the parties who made it? One party to a contract may violate it—break it, so to speak; but does it not require all to lawfully rescind it?

Descending from these general principles, we find the proposition that, in legal contemplation, the Union is perpetual, confirmed by the history of the Union itself. The Union is much older than the Constitution. It was formed in fact, by the Articles of Association in 1774. It was matured and continued by the Declaration of Independence in 1776. *and the faith of all the then thirteen States expressly plighted and engaged that it should be.* It was further matured ~~and expressly declared and pledged to be~~ perpetual, by the Articles of Confederation in 1778. And finally, in 1787, one of the declared objects for ordaining and establishing the Constitution, was *"to form a more perfect union."*

But if destruction of the Union, by one, or by a part only, of the States, be lawfully possible, the Union is *less* perfect than before ~~which was subverting~~ the Constitution, *having lost the vital element of perpetuity—*

It follows from these views that no State, upon its own mere motion, can lawfully get out of the Union,—that *resolves* and *ordinances* to that effect are legally *void;* and that acts of violence, within any State or States, against the authority of the United States, are insurrectionary or *revolutionary* according to circumstances.

4

I therefore consider that the Union is unbroken; and, to the extent of my ability,
I shall take care that the laws of the Union be faithfully executed in all the States.
Doing this I deem to be only a simple duty on my part; and I shall perform it, so far
as practicable, unless my rightful masters, the American people, shall withhold the
requisite means, or, in some ~~authoritative manner~~, direct the contrary. I trust this will not be
regarded as a menace, but only as the declared purpose of the Union that it *will* ~~~~
~~~~ constitutionally defend, and maintain its-
elf —

In doing this there needs to be no bloodshed or violence; and there shall be none,
unless it be forced upon the national authority. ~~All the~~

The power confided to me, will be used to hold,
occupy, and possess the property, and places belonging to the government; and to collect the duties and imposts; but beyond what may be necessary for these objects, there will be no invasion — no using of force against, or among the
people anywhere —

Where hostility to the United States, in any
interior locality, shall be so great and so universal, as to prevent competent resident
citizens from holding the Federal offices, there will be no attempt to force obnoxious
strangers among the people for that object. While the strict legal right may exist
in the government to enforce the exercise of these offices, the attempt to do so would
be so irritating, and so nearly impracticable with all, that I deem it better to forego,
for the time, the uses of such offices.

The mails, unless ~~~~ *repelled*, will continue to be furnished in all parts of the Union.
So far as possible, the people everywhere shall have that sense of perfect security
which is most favorable to calm thought and reflection.

The course here indicated
will be followed, unless current events, and experience, shall show a modification, or change, to
be proper; and in every case and exigency, my
best discretion will be exercised, according to
circumstances actually existing, and with a view
and a hope of a peaceful solution of the national troubles, and the restoration of fraternal
sympathies and affection —

I therefore consider that, in view of the constitution and the laws, the Union is unbroken; and, to the extent of my ability, I shall take care, as the constitution itself expressly enjoins upon me, that the laws of the Union be faithfully executed in all the states.

Doing this I deem to be only a simple duty on my part; and I shall perform it, so far as practicable, unless my rightful masters, the American people, shall withhold the requisite means, or, in some *authoritative manner*, direct the contrary. I trust this will not be regarded as a menace, but only as the declared purpose of the Union that it *will* ~~~~ *constitutionally defend,* and maintain itself—

In doing this there needs to be no bloodshed or violence; and there shall be none, unless it be forced upon the national authority. ~~~~

The power confided to me, will be used to hold, occupy, and possess the property, and places belonging to the government, and to collect the duties and imposts; but beyond what may be necessary for these objects, there will be no invasion— no using of force against, or among the people anywhere.

Where hostility to the United States, in any interior locality, shall be so great and so universal, as to prevent competent resident citizens from holding the Federal offices, there will be no attempt to force obnoxious strangers among the people for that object. While the strict legal right may exist in the government to enforce the exercise of these offices, the attempt to do so would be so irritating, and so nearly impracticable with all, that I deem it better to forego, for the time, the uses of such offices.

The mails, unless *repelled* ~~~~, will continue to be furnished in all parts of the Union. So far as possible, the people everywhere shall have that sense of perfect security which is most favorable to calm thought and reflection.

The course here indicated will be followed, unless current events, and experience, shall show a modification, or change, to be proper; and in every case and exigency, my best discretion will be exercised, according to circumstances actually existing, and with a view and a hope of a peaceful solution of the national troubles, and the restoration of fraternal sympathies and, affections.

e power confided to me, will be used to hold, occupy, and possess the property, and places belonging to the government; and to collect the duties and imposts; but beyond what may be necessary for these objects, there will be no invasion— no using of force against, or among the people anywhere.

Where hostility to the United States, in any interior locality, shall be so great and so universal, as to prevent competent resident citizens from holding the Federal offices, there will be no attempt to force obnoxious strangers among the people for that object. While the strict legal right may exist in the government to enforce the exercise of these offices, the attempt to do so would be so irritating, and so nearly impracticable with all, that I deem it better to forego, for the time, the uses of such offices.

The mails, unless ~~repelled~~ *repelled*, will continue to be furnished in all parts of the Union. So far as possible, the people everywhere shall have that sense of perfect security which is most favorable to calm thought and reflection.

The course here indicated will be followed, unless current events, and experience, shall show a modification, or change, to be proper; and in every case and exigency, my best discretion will be exercised, according to circumstances actually existing, and with a view and a hope of a peaceful solution of the national troubles, and the restoration of fraternal sympathies and affection—

That there are persons who seek to destroy the Union at all events, and are *in one section, or another* glad of any pretext to do it, I will neither affirm or deny; but if there be such, I need address no word to them. To those, however, who really love the Union, may I not speak?

Before entering upon so grave a matter as the destruction of our national ~~Union~~ *fabric, with all its benefits, its memories, and its hopes* would it not be wise to ascertain precisely why we do it? Will you hazard so desperate a step, while there is any possibility that any portion of the ills you fly from have no real existence? Will you, while the certain ills you fly to, are greater than all the real ones you fly from? Will you risk the commission of so fearful a mistake?

~~All profess to be content in the Union, if all constitutional~~ rights can be maintained. Is it true, then, that any right, plainly written in the Constitution, has been denied? I think not. Happily the human mind is so ~~constructed~~ *constituted*, that no party can reach to the audacity of doing this. Think, if you can, of a single instance in

5

which a plainly written provision of the Constitution has ever been denied. If, by the mere force of numbers, a majority should deprive a minority of any clearly written constitutional right, it might, in a moral point of view, justify revolution—certainly would, if such right were a vital one. ~~But~~ such is not our case. All the vital rights of minorities, and of individuals, are so plainly assured to them, by affirmations and *guarantees and prohibitions,* negations in the Constitution, that controversies never arise concerning them. But no organic law can ever be framed with a provision specifically applicable to every question which may occur in practical administration. No foresight can anticipate, nor any document of reasonable length contain express provisions for all possible questions. Shall fugitives from labor be surrendered by national or by State authority? The Constitution does not expressly say. *May* Congress prohibit slavery in the territories? The Constitution does not expressly say. *Must* Congress protect slavery in the territories? The Constitution does not expressly say.

From questions of this class spring all our constitutional controversies, and we divide upon them into majorities and minorities. If the minority will not *acquiesce*, the majority must, or the government must ~~cease~~. There is no other alternative; for continuing the government, is *acquiescence* ~~_____~~ on one side or the other. If a minority, in such case, will secede rather than *acquiesce* ~~_____~~, they make a precedent which, in turn, will divide and ruin them; for a minority of their own ~~_____~~ will secede from them, whenever a majority refuses to be controlled by such minority. ~~_____~~

7742

For instance, why may not any portion of a new confederacy, a year or two hence, arbitrarily secede again, precisely as portions of the present Union now claim to secede from it. All who cherish disunion sentiment, are now being educated to the exact temper of doing this.

Is there such perfect identity of interests among the States to compose a *new* Union, as to produce harmony only, and prevent renewed secession?

7742-B

Plainly, the central idea of secession, is the essence of anarchy.

A majority, held in restraint by constitutional checks, and limitations, and always changing easily, with deliberate changes of popular opinions and sentiments, is the only true sovereign of a free people.

Whoever rejects it, does, of necessity, fly to anarchy or to despotism. Unanimity is impossible; the rule of a minority, as a permanent arrangement, is wholly inadmissable; so that, rejecting the majority principle, anarchy or despotism in some form is all that is left.

I do not forget the position assumed by some, that constitutional questions are to be decided by the Supreme Court; nor do I deny that such decisions must be binding in any case, upon the parties to a suit, as to the object of *that* suit, *while they are also entitled to very high respect and consideration, in all parallel cases, by all other departments of the government.*

7742-C

And while it is obviously possible that such decision may be erroneous in any given case, still the evil effect following it, being limited to that particular case, with the chance that it may be over-ruled, and never become a precedent for other cases, can better be borne than

7742-D

6

practice.

could the greater evils of a different ~~one~~. But if the policy of the government, upon vital questions affecting the whole people, is to be irrevocably fixed by decisions of the Supreme Court, it is plain that the people will have ceased to be their own rulers, having turned their government over to the despotism of the few life-officers composing the Court. Nor is there, in this view, any assault upon the Court or the judges. It is a duty from which they may not shrink, to decide cases properly brought before them; and it is no fault of theirs if others seek to turn their decisions to political purposes.

The Republican party, as I understand, have avowed the purpose to prevent, if they can, the extension of slavery, under the national auspices; and upon this arises the only dispute between the sections.

One section believes slavery is *right*, and ought to be extended, while the other believes it is *wrong*, and ought not to be extended. This is the only substantial dispute. The fugitive slave clause of the Constitution, and the law for the suppression of the foreign slave trade, are each as well enforced, *perhaps*, as any law can ever be in a community where the moral sense of the people *imperfectly supports* the law itself. The great body of the people abide by the dry legal obligation in both cases, and a few break over in each This, I think, cannot be perfectly cured; and it would be worse in both cases *after* the separation of the sections, than before. The foreign slave trade, now imperfectly *ultimately* suppressed, would be revived without restriction, in one section; while fugitive slaves, now only partially surrendered, would not be surrendered at all, by the other.

Physically speaking, we cannot separate. We cannot remove our respective sections from each other, nor build an impassable wall between them. A husband and wife may be divorced, and go out of the presence, and beyond the reach of each other; but the different parts of our country cannot do this. They cannot but remain face to face; and intercourse, either amicable or hostile, must continue between them. Is *possible then* *more* it possible to make that intercourse more advantageous or satisfactory, *after* separation than *before?* Can aliens make treaties easier than friends can make laws? Can treaties be more faithfully enforced between aliens, than laws can among friends? Suppose you go to war, you cannot fight always; and when, after much loss on both sides, and no gain on either, you cease fighting, the identical old questions, as to terms of intercourse, are again upon you.

7743

This country, with its institutions, belongs to the people who inhabit it. Whenever they shall grow weary of the existing government, they can exercise their *constitutional* right of amending it, or their *revolutionary* right to dismember, or overthrow

I can not be ignorant of the fact that many worthy, and patriotic citizens are desirous of having ~~that~~ the national Constitution ~~shall be~~ amended. While I make no recommendation of amendments, I fully recognize the rightful authority of the people over the whole subject, to be exercised in either of the modes prescribed in the instrument itself; and I should, under existing circumstances, favor, rather than oppose, a fair opportunity being afforded the people to act upon it—

could the evils of a different practice. At the same time the candid citizen must confess, that if the policy of the government, upon vital questions, affecting the whole people, is to be irrevocably fixed by decisions of the Supreme Court, the instant they are made, in ordinary litigation between parties, in personal actions, the people will have ceased, to be their own rulers, having, to that extent, practically resigned their government, into the hands of that eminent tribunal. Nor is there, in this view, any assault upon the Court, or the judges. It is a duty, from which they may not shrink, to decide cases properly brought before them; and it is no fault of theirs, if others seek to turn their decisions to political purposes of our country

lieves it is *wrong*, and ought not to be extended. This is the only substantial dispute.

The fugitive slave clause of the Constitution, and the law for the suppression of the foreign slave trade, are each as well enforced, perhaps, as any law can ever be in a community where the moral sense of the people imperfectly supports the law itself. The great body of the people abide by the dry legal obligation in both cases, and a few break over in each. This, I think, cannot be perfectly cured; and it would be worse in both cases *after* the separation of the sections, than before. The foreign slave trade, now imperfectly suppressed, would be ultimately revived without restriction, in one section; while fugitive slaves, now only partially surrendered, would not be surrendered at all, by the other.

Physically speaking, we cannot separate. We cannot remove our respective sections from each other, nor build an impassable wall between them. A husband and wife may be divorced, and go out of the presence, and beyond the reach of each other; but the different parts of our country cannot do this. They cannot but remain face to face; and intercourse, either amicable or hostile, must continue between them. Is it possible then to make that intercourse more advantageous or more satisfactory, *after* separation than *before*? Can aliens make treaties easier than friends can make laws? Can treaties be more faithfully enforced between aliens, than laws can among friends? Suppose you go to war, you cannot fight always; and when, after much loss on both sides, and no gain on either, you cease fighting, the identical old questions, as to terms of intercourse, are again upon you.

7743

This country, with its institutions, belongs to the people who inhabit it. Whenever they shall grow weary of the existing government, they can exercise their *constitutional* right of amending it, or their *revolutionary* right to dismember, or overthrow

I can not be ignorant of the fact that many worthy, and patriotic citizens are desirous of having the national Constitution amended. While I make no recommendation of amendments, I fully recognize the rightful authority of the people over the whole subject, to be exercised in either of the modes prescribed in the instrument itself; and I should, under existing circumstances, favor, rather than oppose, a fair opportunity being afforded the people to act upon it.

7

improved, I make no recommendations of amendments. I am, rather, for the old
ship, and the chart of the old pilots. If, however, the people desire a new, or an
altered vessel, the matter is exclusively their own, and they can move in the premises,
as well without as with an executive recommendation. I shall place no obstacle in the
way of what may appear to be their wishes.

The Chief Magistrate derives all his authority from the people, and they have conferred none upon him to fix terms for the separation of the States. The people themselves can do this *also* if they choose; but the executive, as such, has nothing to do with
it. His duty is to administer the present government, as it came to his hands, and to
transmit it, unimpaired by him, to his successor.

Why should there not be a patient confidence in the ultimate justice of the people?
Is there any better or equal hope, in the world? In our present differences, is either
party without faith *of being* in the right? If the Almighty Ruler of nations, with his eternal
truth and justice, be on *on your side of the North, or on yours of the South,* that truth, and that justice, will surely
prevail, by the judgment of this great tribunal, the American people.

By the frame of the government under which we live, this same people have wisely
given their public servants but little power for mischief: and have, with equal wisdom,
provided for the return of that little to their own hands at very short intervals.
While the people *retain their virtue, and vigilence, no administration*, by any extreme of wickedness or folly, can very seriously injure the
government in the short space of four years.

My countrymen, one and all, *think calmly and* well, upon this whole sub-
ject. Nothing valuable can be lost by taking time. If there be an object to *hurry* any of you, in hot haste,
to a step which you would never take *deliberately*, that object will be frustrated by
taking time; but no good object can be frustrated by it. Such of you as are now
dissatisfied, still have the old Constitution unimpaired, and, on the sensitive point, the
laws of your own framing under it; while the new administration will have no immediate power, if it would, to change either. If it were admitted that you who are
dissatisfied, hold the right side in the dispute, there still is no single good reason for
precipitate action. Intelligence, patriotism, Christianity, and a firm reliance on Him,
who has never yet forsaken this favored land, are still competent to adjust, in the best
way, all our present difficulty.

In *your* hands, my dissatisfied fellow countrymen, and not in *mine*, is the momentous issue of civil war. The government will not assail *you*.
You can have no conflict, without being yourselves the aggressors. *You* have no oath
registered in Heaven to destroy the government, while *I* shall have the most solemn one
to "preserve, protect and defend" it.

I am loth to close. We are not enemies,
but friends— We must not be enemies. Though passion may
have strained, it must not break our bonds of affection.
The mystic chords of memory, stretching from every battle-
field, and patriot grave, to every living heart and hearth-
stone, all over this broad land, will yet swell the chorus of the Union, when again touched, as surely they will
be, by the better angels of our nature.

7744

I will venture to add that, to me, the Convention mode seems preferable, in that it allows amendments to originate with the people themselves, instead of only permitting them to take, or reject, propositions, originated by others, not especially chosen for the purpose, and which might not be precisely such, as they would wish to either accept or refuse.

which amendment, however, I have not seen, I understand a proposed amendment to the constitution, has passed Congress, to the effect that the federal government, shall never interfere with the domestic institutions of the States, including that of persons held to service — To avoid misconstruction of what I have said, I depart from my purpose not to speak of particular amendments, so far as to say that, holding such a provision to now be implied Constitutional law, I have no objection to its being made express, and irrevocable —

774 2

laws of your own framing under it; while the new administration will have no immediate power, if it would, to change either. If it were admitted that you who are dissatisfied, hold the right side in the dispute, there still is no single good reason for precipitate action. Intelligence, patriotism, Christianity, and a firm reliance on Him, who has never yet forsaken this favored land, are still competent to adjust, in the best way, all our present difficulty.

In *your* hands, my dissatisfied fellow countrymen, and not in *mine*, is the momentous issue of civil war. The government will not assail *you*. ~~...~~ You can have no conflict, without being yourselves the aggressors. *You* have no oath registered in Heaven to destroy the government, while *I* shall have the most solemn one to "preserve, protect and defend" it.

7744

I am loth to close. We are not enemies, but friends — We must not be enemies. Though passion may have strained, it must not break our bonds of affection. The mystic chords of memory, stretching from every battle-field, and patriot grave, to every living heart and hearth-stone, all over this broad land, will yet swell the chorus of the Union, when again touched, as surely they will be, by the better angels of our nature.

FINAL CORRECTED DRAFT
OF THE
FIRST INAUGURAL ADDRESS OF
PRESIDENT ABRAHAM LINCOLN

Delivered at the
United States Capitol, Washington, D.C.
March 4, 1861

In compliance with a custom as old as the government itself, I appear before page 1 you to address you briefly, and to take, in your presence, the oath prescribed by the Constitution of the United States, to be taken by the President "before he enters on the execution of his office."

I do not consider it necessary, at present, for me to discuss those matters of administration about which there is no special anxiety, or excitement.

Apprehension seems to exist among the people of the Southern States, that by the accession of a Republican Administration, their property, and their peace, and personal security, are to be endangered. There has never been any reasonable cause for such apprehension. Indeed, the most ample evidence to the contrary has all the while existed, and been open to their inspection. It is found in nearly all the published speeches of him who now addresses you. I do but quote from one of those speeches when I declare that "I have no purpose, directly or indirectly, to interfere with the institution of slavery in the States where it exists. I believe I have no lawful right to do so, and I have no inclination to do so." Those who nominated and elected me did so with full knowledge that I had made this, and many similar declarations, and had never recanted them. And more than this, they placed in the platform, for my acceptance, and as a law to themselves, and to me, the clear and emphatic resolution which I now read:

"*Resolved,* That the maintenance inviolate of the rights of the States, and especially the right of each State to order and control its own domestic institutions according to its own judgment exclusively, is essential to that balance of power on which the perfection and endurance of our political fabric depend; and we denounce the lawless invasion by armed force of the soil of any State or Territory, no matter under what pretext, as among the gravest of crimes."

page 2

I now reiterate these sentiments: and in doing so, I only press upon the public attention the most conclusive evidence of which the case is susceptible, that the property, peace and security of no section are to be in anywise endangered by the now incoming Administration. I add too, that all the protection which, consistently with the Constitution and the laws, can be given, will be cheerfully given to all the States when lawfully demanded, for whatever cause—as cheerfully to one section, as to another.

There is much controversy about the delivering up of fugitives from service or labor. The clause I now read is as plainly written in the Constitution as any other of its provisions:

"No person held to service or labor in one State, under the laws thereof, escaping into another, shall, in consequence of any law or regulation therein, be discharged from such service or labor, but shall be delivered up on claim of the party to whom such service or labor may be due."

It is scarcely questioned that this provision was intended by those who made it, for the reclaiming of what we call fugitive slaves; and the intention of the law-giver is the law. All members of Congress swear their support to the whole Constitution—to this provision as much as to any other. To the proposition, then, that slaves whose cases come within the terms of this clause, "shall be delivered up," their oaths are unanimous. Now, if they would make the effort in good temper, could they not, with nearly equal unanimity, frame and pass a law, by means of which to keep good that unanimous oath?

There is some difference of opinion whether this clause should be enforced by national or by state authority; but surely that difference is not a very material one. If the slave is to be surrendered, it can be of but little consequence to him, or to others, by which authority it is done. And should any one, in any case, be content that his oath shall go unkept, on a merely unsubstantial controversy as to *how* it shall be kept?

Again, in any law upon this subject, ought not all the safeguards of liberty known in civilized and humane jurisprudence to be introduced, so that a free man be not, in any case, surrendered as a slave? And might it not be well, at the same time, to provide by law for the enforcement of that clause in the Constitution which guarranties that "The citizens of each State shall be entitled to all previleges and immunities of citizens in the several States"?

I take the official oath to-day, with no mental reservations, and with no purpose to construe the Constitution or laws, by any hypercritical rules. And while I do not choose to specify particular acts of Congress as proper to be enforced, I do suggest, that it will be much safer for all, both in official and private stations, to conform to, and abide by, all those acts which stand unrepealed, than to violate any of them, trusting to find impunity in having them held to be unconstitutional.

It is seventy-two years since the first inauguration of a President under our national Constitution. During that period fifteen different and greatly distinguished citizens, have, in succession, administered the executive branch of the government. They have conducted it through many perils; and, generally, with great success. Yet, with all this scope for precedent, I now enter upon the same task for the brief constitutional term of four years, under great and peculiar difficulty. A disruption of the Federal Union heretofore only menaced, is now formidably attempted.

page 3

I hold, that in contemplation of universal law, and of the Constitution, the Union of these States is perpetual. Perpetuity is implied, if not expressed, in the fundamental law of all national governments. It is safe to assert that no government proper, ever had a provision in its organic law for its own termination. Continue to execute all the express provisions of our national Constitution, and the Union will endure forever—it being impossible to destroy it, except by some action not provided for in the instrument itself.

Again, if the United States be not a government proper, but an association of States in the nature of contract merely, can it, as a contract, be peaceably unmade, by less than all the parties who made it? One party to a contract may violate it—break it, so to speak; but does it not require all to lawfully rescind it?

Descending from these general principles, we find the proposition that, in legal contemplation, the Union is perpetual, confirmed by the history of the Union itself. The Union is much older than the Constitution. It was formed in fact, by the Articles of Association in 1774. It was matured and continued by the Declaration of Independence in 1776. It was further matured and the faith of all the then thirteen States expressly plighted and engaged that it should be perpetual, by the Articles of Confederation in 1778. And finally, in 1787, one of the declared objects for ordaining and establishing the Constitution, was "*to form a more perfect Union.*"

But if destruction of the Union, by one, or by a part only, of the States, be lawfully possible, the Union is *less* perfect than before the Constitution, having lost the vital element of perpetuity.

It follows from these views that no State, upon its own mere motion, can lawfully get out of the Union,—that *resolves* and *ordinances* to that effect are legally void; and that acts of violence, within any State or States, against the authority of the United States, are insurrectionary or revolutionary, according to circumstances.

page 4

I therefore consider that, in view of the Constitution and the laws, the Union is unbroken; and to the extent of my ability, I shall take care, as the constitution itself expressly enjoins upon me, that the laws of the Union be faithfully executed in all the States. Doing this I deem to be only a simple duty on my part; and I shall perform it, so far as practicable, unless my rightful masters, the American people, shall withhold the requisite means, or, in some authoritative manner, direct the contrary. I trust this will not be regarded as a menace, but only as the declared purpose of the Union that it *will* constitutionally defend, and maintain itself.

In doing this there needs to be no bloodshed or violence; and there shall be none, unless it be forced upon the national authority. The power confided to me, will be used to hold, occupy, and possess the property, and places belonging to the government, and to collect the duties and imposts; but beyond what may be necessary for these objects, there will be no invasion—no using of force against, or among the people anywhere. Where hostility to the United States, in any interior locality, shall be so great and so universal, as to prevent competent resident citizens from holding the Federal offices, there will be no attempt to force obnoxious strangers among the people for that object. While the strict legal right may exist in the government to enforce the exercise of these offices, the attempt to do so would be so irritating, and so nearly impracticable with all, that I deem it better to forego, for the time, the uses of such offices.

The mails, unless repelled, will continue to be furnished in all parts of the Union. So far as possible, the people everywhere shall have that sense of perfect security which is most favorable to calm thought and reflection. The course here indicated will be followed, unless current events, and experience, shall show a modification, or change, to be proper; and in every case and exigency, my best discretion will be exercised, according to circumstances actually existing, and with a view and a hope of a peaceful solution of the national troubles, and the restoration of fraternal sympathies and affections.

That there are persons in one section, or another who seek to destroy the Union at all events, and are glad of any pretext to do it, I will neither affirm or deny; but if there be such, I need address no word to them. To those, however, who really love the Union, may I not speak?

Before entering upon so grave a matter as the destruction of our national fabric, with all its benefits, its memories, and its hopes, would it not be wise to ascertain precisely why we do it? Will you hazard so desperate a step, while there is any possibility that any portion of the ills you fly from, have no real existence? Will you, while the certain ills you fly to, are greater than all the real ones you fly from? Will you risk the commission of so fearful a mistake?

All profess to be content in the Union, if all constitutional rights can be maintained. Is it true, then, that any right, plainly written in the Constitution, has been denied? I think not. Happily the human mind is so constituted, that no party can reach to the audacity of doing this. Think, if you can, of a single instance in which a plainly written provision of the Constitution has ever been denied. If, by the mere force of numbers, a majority should deprive a minority of any clearly written constitutional right, it might, in a moral point of view, justify revolution—certainly would, if such right were a vital one. But such is not our case. All the vital rights of minorities, and of individuals, are so plainly assured to them, by affirmations and negations, guarranties and prohibitions, in the Constitution, that controversies never arise concerning them. But no organic law can ever be framed with a provision specifically applicable to every question which may occur in practical administration. No foresight can anticipate, nor any document of reasonable length contain express provisions for all possible questions. Shall fugitives from labor be surrendered by national or by State authority? The Constitution does not expressly say. *May* Congress prohibit slavery in the territories? The Constitution does not expressly say. *Must* Congress protect slavery in the territories? The Constitution does not expressly say.

From questions of this class spring all our constitutional controversies, and we divide upon them into majorities and minorities. If the minority will not acquiesce, the majority must, or the government must cease. There is no other alternative; for continuing the government, is acquiescence on one side or the other. If a minority, in such case, will secede rather than acquiesce, they make a precedent which, in turn, will divide and ruin them; for a minority of their own will secede from them, whenever a majority refuses to be controlled by such minority. For instance, why may not any portion of a new confederacy, a year or two hence, arbitrarily secede again, precisely as portions of the present Union now claim to secede from it. All who cherish disunion sentiments, are now being educated to the exact temper of doing this. Is there such perfect identity of interests among the States to compose a new Union, as to produce harmony only, and prevent renewed secession?

Plainly, the central idea of secession, is the essence of anarchy. A majority, held in restraint by constitutional checks, and limitations, and always changing easily, with deliberate changes of popular opinions and sentiments, is the only true sovereign of a free people. Whoever rejects it, does, of necessity, fly to anarchy or to despotism. Unanimity is impossible; the rule of a minority, as a permanent arrangement, is wholly inadmissible; so that, rejecting the majority principle, anarchy, or despotism in some form, is all that is left.

I do not forget the position assumed by some, that constitutional questions are to be decided by the Supreme Court; nor do I deny that such decisions must be binding in any case, upon the parties to a suit, as to the object of that suit, while they are also entitled to very high respect and consideration, in all paralel cases, by all other departments of the government. And while it is obviously possible that such decision may be erroneous in any given case, still the evil effect following it, being limited to that particular case, with the chance that it may be over-ruled, and never become a precedent for other cases, can better be borne than could the evils of a different practice. At the same time the candid page 6 citizen must confess, that if the policy of the government, upon vital questions, affecting the whole people, is to be irrevocably fixed by decisions of the Supreme Court, the instant they are made, in ordinary litigation between parties, in personal actions, the people will have ceased, to be their own rulers, having, to that extent, practically resigned their government, into the hands of that eminent tribunal. Nor is there, in this view, any assault upon the Court, or the judges. It is a duty, from which they may not shrink, to decide cases properly brought before them; and it is no fault of theirs, if others seek to turn their decisions to political purposes.

One section of our country believes slavery is *right*, and ought to be extended, while the other believes it is *wrong*, and ought not to be extended.

This is the only substantial dispute. The fugitive slave clause of the Constitution, and the law for the suppression of the foreign slave trade, are each as well enforced, perhaps, as any law can ever be in a community where the moral sense of the people imperfectly supports the law itself. The great body of the people abide by the dry legal obligation in both cases, and a few break over in each. This, I think, cannot be perfectly cured; and it would be worse in both cases *after* the separation of the sections, than before. The foreign slave trade, now imperfectly suppressed, would be ultimately revived without restriction, in one section; while fugitive slaves, now only partially surrendered, would not be surrendered at all, by the other.

Physically speaking, we cannot separate. We cannot remove our respective sections from each other, nor build an impassable wall between them. A husband and wife may be divorced, and go out of the presence, and beyond the reach of each other; but the different parts of our country cannot do this. They cannot but remain face to face; and intercourse, either amicable or hostile, must continue between them. Is it possible then to make that intercourse more advantageous, or more satisfactory, *after* separation than *before*? Can aliens make treaties easier than friends can make laws? Can treaties be more faithfully enforced between aliens, than laws can among friends? Suppose you go to war, you cannot fight always; and when, after much loss on both sides, and no gain on either, you cease fighting, the identical old questions, as to terms of intercourse, are again upon you.

This country, with its institutions, belongs to the people who inhabit it. Whenever they shall grow weary of the existing government, they can exercise their *constitutional* right of amending it, or their *revolutionary* right to dismember, or overthrow it. I can not be ignorant of the fact that many worthy, and patriotic citizens are desirous of having the national constitution amended. While I make no recommendation of amendments, I fully recognize the rightful authority of the people over the whole subject, to be exercised in either of the modes prescribed in the instrument itself; and I should, under existing circumstances, favor, rather than oppose, a fair oppertunity being afforded the people to act upon it.

I will venture to add that, to me, the convention mode seems preferable, in that it allow amendments to originate with the people themselves, instead of only permitting them to take, or reject, propositions, originated by others, not especially chosen for the purpose, and which might not be precisely such, as they would wish to either accept or refuse. I understand a proposed amendment to the Constitution—which amendment, however, I have not seen, has passed Congress, to the effect that the federal government, shall never interfere with the domestic institutions of the States, including that of persons held to service. To avoid misconstruction of what I have said, I depart from my purpose not to speak of particular amendments, so far as to say that, holding such a provision to now be implied constitutional law, I have no objection to its being made express, and irrevocable.

The Chief Magistrate derives all his authority from the people, and they have conferred none upon him to fix terms for the separation of the States. The people themselves can do this also if they choose; but the executive, as such, has nothing to do with it. His duty is to administer the present government, as it came to his hands, and to transmit it, unimpaired by him, to his successor.

Why should there not be a patient confidence in the ultimate justice of the people? Is there any better, or equal hope, in the world? In our present differences, is either party without faith of being in the right? If the Almighty Ruler of nations, with his eternal truth and justice, be on your side of the North, or on yours of the South, that truth, and that justice, will surely prevail, by the judgment of this great tribunal, the American people.

By the frame of the government under which we live, this same people have wisely given their public servants but little power for mischief; and have, with equal wisdom, provided for the return of that little to their own hands at very short intervals.

While the people retain their virtue, and vigilence, no administration, by any extreme of wickedness or folly, can very seriously injure the government, in the short space of four years.

My countrymen, one and all, think calmly and *well*, upon this whole subject. Nothing valuable can be lost by taking time. If there be an object to *hurry* any of you, in hot haste, to a step which you would never take *deliberately*, that object will be frustrated by taking time; but no good object can be frustrated by it. Such of you as are now dissatisfied, still have the old Constitution unimpaired, and, on the sensitive point, the laws of your own framing under it; while the new administration will have no immediate power, if it would, to change either. If it were admitted that you who are dissatisfied, hold the right side in the dispute, there still is no single good reason for precipitate action. Intelligence, patriotism, Christianity, and a firm reliance on Him, who has never yet forsaken this favored land, are still competent to adjust, in the best way, all our present difficulty.

In *your* hands, my dissatisfied fellow countrymen, and not in *mine*, is the momentous issue of civil war. The government will not assail *you*. You can have no conflict, without being yourselves the aggressors. *You* have no oath registered in Heaven to destroy the government, while *I* shall have the most solemn one to "preserve, protect and defend" it.

I am loth to close. We are not enemies, but friends. We must not be enemies. Though passion may have strained, it must not break our bonds of affection. The mystic chords of memory, stretching from every battle-field, and patriot grave, to every living heart and hearthstone, all over this broad land, will yet swell the chorus of the Union, when again touched, as surely they will be, by the better angels of our nature.

SOURCES AND CREDITS

Facsimile of the sums book (frontispiece) is courtesy of The Lincoln Museum, Fort Wayne, Indiana.

Facsimiles of the pages from Lincoln's copy of *The Life and Speeches of Henry Clay* (pages xiv and xv) are courtesy of The Lincoln Museum, Fort Wayne, Indiana.

Facsimile of the letter dated Feb. 14, 1860 from Abraham Lincoln (Appendix I) is courtesy of Department of Special Collections and University Archives, Stanford University Libraries.

Facsimiles of the final corrected proofs of Lincoln's first inaugural address (Appendix II) are courtesy of the Library of Congress, Manuscript Division, Robert Todd Lincoln Collection of Abraham Lincoln Papers.

· · · · · · · · · ·

Transcriptions of the letter of Feb. 14, 1860 and of the final text of the first inaugural address, incorporating Lincoln's handwritten changes, were verified to those contained in *The Collected Works of Abraham Lincoln*: The Abraham Lincoln Association, Springfield, Illinois, vols. 3 and 4, edited by Roy B. Basler (New Brunswick: Rutgers University Press, 1953).

The poem that accompanies the image of Lincoln's sums book (frontispiece) is transcribed as it appears in *The Wit and Wisdom of Abraham Lincoln*, compiled by Bill Adler (New York: Carol Publishing Group, 1993).

ACKNOWLEDGMENTS

Finding Lincoln is a challenging task. Like the pennies that bear his image, Lincoln's documents are scattered far and wide, then sometimes, it seems, buried.

Our great good fortune was finding Dr. Daniel Stowell of The Papers of Abraham Lincoln Project, who was generous beyond measure with his assistance. At the Library of Congress, we also discovered two treasures, Dr. John Sellers and Bonnie Coles.

Cindy VanHorn of The Lincoln Museum, Mattie Taormina and Polly Armstrong of the Stanford University Libraries, and Jennifer Ericson of the Abraham Lincoln Presidential Library offered their help willingly and graciously. We are grateful to them, and to the many other keepers of the Lincoln flame whom we encountered along the way.

ABOUT OUR CONTRIBUTOR

Ronald C. White, Jr. is the author of *Lincoln's Greatest Speech: The Second Inaugural*, a New York Times Notable Book of 2002, and *The Eloquent President: A Portrait of Lincoln Through His Words*, a Book-of-the-Month Club selection. He has lectured on Lincoln to audiences at Gettysburg, the Library of Congress, and the White House.

Dr. White is Professor Emeritus of American Intellectual and Religious History at San Francisco Theological Seminary, a Visiting Professor of History at UCLA, and a Fellow at the Huntington Library in Pasadena. His newest book is *A. Lincoln: A Biography* (Random House, 2009).

UNCOMMON BOOKS
FOR SERIOUS READERS

A Boy at the Hogarth Press
Written and illustrated by
Richard Kennedy

The Dream
Sir Winston Churchill

A Fortnight in the Wilderness
Alexis de Tocqueville

The Grimani Breviary
Foreword by Ross King

**Jerusalem: The Saga of
the Holy City**
Benjamin Mazar et al.

**The Little Guide to Your
Well-Read Life**
Steve Leveen

The Making of The Finest Hour
Speech by Winston S. Churchill
Introduction by
Richard M. Langworth

New York
Theodore Roosevelt

Notes on Our Times
E. B. White

On a Life Well Spent
Cicero
Preface by Benjamin Franklin

Painting as a Pastime
Winston S. Churchill

Samuel Johnson's Dictionary
Selections from the 1755 work
that defined the English language
Edited by Jack Lynch

Samuel Johnson's Insults
Edited by Jack Lynch

The Silverado Squatters
Six selected chapters
Robert Louis Stevenson

**Sir Winston Churchill's Life
Through His Paintings**
David Coombs
with Minnie Churchill
Foreword by Mary Soames

Levenger Press is the publishing arm of

LEVENGER®
TOOLS FOR SERIOUS READERS

Levengerpress.com   800.544.0880

practice.

could the greater evils of a different ~~one~~. But if the policy of the government, upon vital questions affecting the whole people, is to be irrevocably fixed by decisions of the Supreme Court, it is plain that the people will have ceased to be their own rulers, having turned their government over to the despotism of the few life-officers composing the Court. Nor is there, in this view, any assault upon the Court or the judges. It is a duty from which they may not shrink, to decide cases properly brought before them; and it is no fault of theirs if others seek to turn their decisions to political purposes.

☞ The Republican party, as I understand, have avowed the purpose to prevent, if they can, the extension of slavery, under the national auspices; and upon this arises the only dispute between the sections.

One section believes slavery is *right*, and ought to be extended, while the other believes it is *wrong*, and ought not to be extended. This is the only substantial dispute. The fugitive slave clause of the Constitution, and the law for the suppression of the foreign slave trade, are each as well enforced, *perhaps*, as any law can ever be in a community where the moral sense of the people ~~imperfectly~~ *imperfectly supports* the law itself. The great body of the people abide by the dry legal obligation in both cases, and a few break over in each This, I think, cannot be perfectly cured; and it would be worse in both cases *after* the separation of the sections, than before. The foreign slave trade, now imperfectly suppressed, would be *ultimately* revived without restriction, in one section; while fugitive slaves, now only partially surrendered, would not be surrendered at all, by the other.

Physically speaking, we cannot separate. We cannot remove our respective sections from each other, nor build an impassable wall between them. A husband and wife may be divorced, and go out of the presence, and beyond the reach of each other; but the different parts of our country cannot do this. They cannot but remain face to face; and intercourse, either amicable or hostile, must continue between them. Is it ~~possible then~~ possible to make that intercourse more advantageous or *more* satisfactory, *after* separation than *before?* Can aliens make treaties easier than friends can make laws? Can treaties be more faithfully enforced between aliens, than laws can among friends? Suppose you go to war, you cannot fight always; and when, after much loss on both sides, and no gain on either, you cease fighting, the identical old questions, as to terms of intercourse, are again upon you.

☞ This country, with its institutions, belongs to the people who inhabit it. Whenever they shall grow weary of the existing government, they can exercise their *constitutional* right of amending it, or their *revolutionary* right to dismember, or overthrow

I can not be ignorant of the fact that many worthy, and patriotic citizens are desirous *having* ~~that~~ the national Constitution ~~should be~~ amended. While I make no recommendation of amendments, I fully recognize the rightful authority of the people over the *whole* subject, to be exercised in either of the modes prescribed in the instrument itself; and I should, under existing circumstances, favor, rather than oppose, a fair opportunity being afforded the people to act upon it.